Searching the Globe for Answers

Searching the Globe for Answers

Preparing and Supporting School Leaders

Edited by Peter R. Litchka

ROWMAN & LITTLEFIELD
Lanham • Boulder • New York • London

Published by Rowman & Littlefield
An imprint of Rowman & Littlefield Publishing Group, Inc.
4501 Forbes Boulevard, Suite 200, Lanham, Maryland 20706
www.rowman.com

6 Tinworth Street, London SE11 5AL, United Kingdom

Copyright © 2019 by Peter R. Litchka

All rights reserved. No part of this book may be reproduced in any form or by any electronic or mechanical means, including information storage and retrieval systems, without written permission from the publisher, except by a reviewer who may quote passages in a review.

British Library Cataloguing in Publication Information Available

Library of Congress Cataloging-in-Publication Data Available

ISBN 978-1-4758-5293-6 (cloth)
ISBN 978-1-4758-5294-3 (pbk.)
ISBN 978-1-4758-5295-0 (electronic)

To Ed Davis, Greg Eckles, and Don Vetter (dec.), three extraordinary school leaders, who throughout their careers inspired, empowered, challenged, and recognized educators to be the best so that all young people could succeed.

School Leadership Matters!
Children and young people in schools around the world will graduate to face a very different future from previous generations. Technological advances and scientific discovery are significantly accelerating the amount of knowledge and information available. We now live in an increasingly interdependent international community, where success or failure in one country has consequences for many others.

There is a growing concern that the role of school principal, designed for the industrial age, has not evolved to deal with the complex challenges that schools are preparing children and young people to face in the 21st century. As expectations of what school leaders should achieve change, so must the definition and distribution of school leadership roles.

—Pont, Nusche, and Moorman (Eds.), 2007[1]

Why Would Such a Talented Principal Choose to Leave the Job?
Boxes crowd the hallways, moving in and moving out. I'm in an empty office at Animo Phyllis Wheatley Middle School in South L.A. talking to Principal Nat Pickering, who has resigned after three years so that he can go back to being a teacher. Back when I was teaching, I worked with him; he was a history teacher for years before he became principal of our school. I will forever be indebted to Nat, who despite being insanely busy, voluntarily met with me two or three times a month to coach me on the plethora of problems I was having in my various classes; he helped me shape my curriculum, talked me through issues with students and, more times than I can count, simply listened to me venting.

---

[1] OECD Publishing. (2009). *Improving school leadership-The toolkit.* Paris, France: Author.

Now, after three years as Principal at Wheatley, he's leaving the job to go back to being a classroom teacher. By all accounts, his stint at the school has been successful.

—Valerie Strauss, 2015[2]

---

2   Straus, V. (2015, February 10). Why a great principal burned out-what could have prevented it. *Washington Post*. Retrieved from https://www.washingtonpost.com/news/answer-sheet/wp/2015/02/10/

Contents

Preface　　xi

Acknowledgments　　xv

1 School Leadership or School Management?: Reflections from a Polish Perspective　　1
Rafał Piwowarski

2 The Australian Education Revolution: The Impact of a Reform Movement on School Leadership and System Performance　　20
Jack Rice and Justin Garrick

3 School Leadership in Ethiopia: Reinventing the Principalship through Locally Responsive Practices　　39
Abebayehu Tekleselassie and Amaarah DeCuir

4 Principals' Taking Initiative Level and School Circumstances in Turkey　　58
Emine Babaoğlan

About the Authors　　77

About the Editor　　79

Preface

HELP WANTED

The New Millennium School District is accepting applications for the position of school principal. The following qualifications and areas of expertise are required:

At least 10 years of successful teaching. Master's degree or equivalent in educational leadership. Hold a current leadership certification from the educational governing agency. Have the knowledge, understanding, and experience as an instructional leader.

Have the ability to effectively manage human, physical, and financial resources in support of the school's mission. Be a facilitator of effective change. Be collaborative, inspirational, and empowering. Be an effective listener. Put the needs of students first in terms of their academic and personal growth. Model appropriate professional and ethical behaviors. Be the teachers' teacher.

When reviewing the aforementioned job description for the position of school principal, it appears this school is looking for a leader who is "perfect" in all aspects of leadership and management. And while it could be argued that each of the descriptors is an essential requirement of a school leader in the twenty-first century, it could also be argued that what is being asked for would require a leader who has an infinite amount of wisdom, energy, and confidence, as well as an inordinate amount of resources and support from the local educational governing agency.

In view of the ever-increasing demands for school leaders to enhance and ensure that the teaching-learning equation is the focal point of all leadership and management activities, there has been an increased emphasis on such school leadership, particularly in terms of the principal being *the* instructional leader throughout the world. Acknowledging differences in culture and traditions within countries and regions of the world, a number of nations have earnestly subscribed to a more modern definition of school leadership, placing more emphasis on instructional and collaborative leadership and less on the managerial side, while other nations may continue to hold onto the traditional role of the principal as *the* manager of the school.

Even for those countries that espouse the concept of the principal being the *instructional leader first and manager second*, school leaders with such intentions are often faced with what Andy Hargreaves and Dean Fink referred to as *Fast-School Nations*, where schools (and school districts) place themselves on a treadmill of short-term achievement targets, repetitive changes, top-down and out-of-touch decision-making, blaming, and shaming, leading to frustrated and less effective school leaders and teachers (Hargreaves & Fink, 2005).

There is also the issue of gender and school leadership, which has been written about extensively over the past several decades. And while the percentage of school leaders who are female continues to rise, the real issue is that of role expectations. I have spoken to numerous school principals from Israel, Poland, and Turkey over the past decade, and in just about every discussion, these principals share the dilemma of how they are expected to lead (don't be too assertive), how they are expected to take care of the school during the day and their own children and home during the evening, and how they, as females, are considered to be strong in the area of instruction, but not so much in the managerial part of leading a school. And, according to these principals, the fact is, there are many males who do not like to work for a female principal.

We also may wish to think about the extraordinary challenges facing school principals who have high levels of student poverty, less financial and human resources, and in many cases, more government oversight than others that have less poverty and more resources. The issue then becomes, should all current and aspiring school leaders be trained in the same manner, using similar theories and practices as a foundation, or should the professional development be based more on student and community demographics?

As we think about both the "Help Wanted" message and the characteristics of *Fast-School Nations*, it is obvious that if the role of the school leader is to be, then the training for aspiring school leaders and the continuous professional development of current school leaders needs to be based upon a *clear* and *concise* understanding of the overall aims of education in general, and what the overall teaching-learning process needs to look like in achieving this. Then, and only then, can the conceptualization be developed as to what the knowledge, understandings, abilities, and leadership skills, traits, and behaviors are required of school leaders.

In chapter 1, "School Leadership or School Management?: Reflections from a Polish Perspective," Rafał Piwowarski presents an appraisal of how Poland is attempting to reimagine the roles and responsibilities of the school principal in terms of leader versus manager, collaborator versus authoritarian, and leadership styles that may be more effective than others.

In chapter 2, "The Australian Education Revolution: The Impact of a Reform Movement on School Leadership and System Performance," Jack Rice and Justin Garrick consider the impact of the educational policy transformation that occurred across Australia (2008–2013) in light of the expectations, challenges, outcomes, and future direction of education in Australia, including the role of school leaders.

In chapter 3, "School Leadership in Ethiopia: Reinventing the Principalship through Locally Responsive Practices," Abebayehu Tekleselassie and Amaarah DeCuir provide an overview of school leadership development in Ethiopia, including the challenges faced regarding the types of professional development needed, who would be making such decisions, and how resources would be garnered and allocated. The authors posit that, in spite of these concerns/issues, local school principals in many areas have "reinvented" the role of the school principal through collaboration and professional learning.

The final chapter of this section, "Principals in Turkey Using Initiative in Relation to School Context and Circumstances," is from Emine Babaoğlan of Turkey, who examines the extent in which principals in Turkey consider using their own resourcefulness and inventiveness to improve how they lead their faculty, students, and community.

REFERENCE

Hargreaves, A. and Fink, D. (2005). *Sustainable leadership*. San Francisco: Jossey-Bass.

Acknowledgments

I wish to thank the International Society for Educational Planning (ISEP), of which I have been a member since 2006. ISEP has a commitment to healthy and pertinent discourse regarding education, and this commitment first and foremost is of a global nature. Without ISEP, I doubt I would have not only been able to travel to countries such as Cyprus, Hungary, Israel, Poland, and Turkey, but of more importance, I would not have been able to meet educators from these and other countries in a professional and collegial manner. And thank you to Walter Polka, my friend and mentor, who encouraged me to join ISEP back in 2006.

I express my deep gratitude to Stephanie Dunford for her keen editorial sense and critique in the development of this book. Her insights, questions, critiques, and reviews were most helpful. And, to all of the school leaders in Israel, Poland, Turkey, and other nations for whom I have had the distinct opportunity to interact with. The passion demonstrated by such leaders is truly amazing. Thank you for what you do!

Chapter One

School Leadership or School Management?

Reflections from a Polish Perspective

Rafał Piwowarski

The increased interest in school leadership seen in recent years provides arguments for finding that there is a feedback loop between practice affecting theory, used and reinforced at the same time by politics. On the one hand, theory and research provide justifications for decision-makers in accordance with the principle of *evidence-based policy*. On the other hand, decision-makers (education authorities in countries, European Union institutions, and international organizations) define goals and allocate funds for specific initiatives (e.g., cooperation networks and structural programs) and research activity directed at a particular types of leadership (Hernik, Wasilewska, & Kasprzak, 2012, p. 13).

Attaching more and more importance to school leadership, considerations must be made at various levels; education policy or school practice is a pragmatic challenge focused on what is happening at school, in the environment it operates, the education system, at the country level, international organization level, or union of countries. The goals in each case are similar:

> through proper school leadership, building a school environment that is conducive to learning and teaching, thus, improving the didactic and educational effectiveness of the school and the teacher.

Behind these beliefs, in many cases, there are additional important factors, such as expenditure on education and the condition of the labor market; it is also about economic efficiency and better adjustment of education to the economy. However, better learning outcomes can be achieved by enhancing the professionalism of teachers, including educational leaders.

Activities of the European Union and individual countries focus on the central role of school leadership in creating school environments conducive to adopting effective attitudes toward teaching and learning. The Communication from the Commission of Education of November 2012 (European Commission, 2012) contained proposals for investing in education and training and formulated a clear message aimed at *supporting school leadership for achieving better educational outcomes of schools* (author emphasis).

Based on the Communication, the Council of Europe conclusions were adopted focusing on the promotion of innovative leadership, as well as the introduction of innovation in education through better leadership. It is worth emphasizing that these conclusions translate into three distinctive challenges facing the European Union and its member states:

First, promoting new approaches to leadership for creating innovative school environments. This challenge, not without reason, presupposes that the key factor of change is the school leader, the school principal. The Eurydice report (EACEA: Education, Audiovisual and Culture Executive Agency/Key Data, 2013) gives an example of the Finnish school, which among other things is characterized by a high degree of flexibility in innovative leadership solutions, such as setting up or disbanding groups of leaders depending on current school needs. Only new leadership initiatives can unleash bottom-up change initiatives undertaken by teachers.

The second challenge is to *make school leadership more attractive*. As early as 2009, education ministers deemed it necessary to redefine the role of managing educational institutions and to free school leaders from the main administrative burdens. The attractiveness of the school principal's position should be recognized in the context of the possibilities of European systems to train, recruit, and hire the right people to fulfill leadership roles.

This is particularly important when, in most countries, the majority of principals are over fifty years old and when only one candidate applies for the vacant post of school's head (EACEA/Key Data, work cited). The Eurydice report (2013) also drew attention to the huge diversity in the member states in terms of the length and content of the courses preparing for the role of principal. There are countries where no compulsory forms of training were required in this area (five years of teaching experience, however, was necessary; this was true for fifteen countries among others: Belgium/Flanders, Bulgaria, Denmark, Ireland, Greece, Latvia, Hungary, Scotland, Norway) and those in which this period of training lasted from six to eighteen months (England six to eighteen months, France twelve months).

In Poland, 210 hours was required, including only twenty-six hours related to management. This diversity may hide untapped potential for cooperation and exchange of best practices in the field of leadership. In some countries, the dramatic decline in women's participation in school management is also observed, especially at higher school levels in the Czech Republic, Germany, England, Finland, Sweden, and Norway.

Supporting new solutions in the field of effective and responsible school autonomy was the third challenge in educational leadership as formulated by the secretariat of the Council of Europe for the European Commissioner for Education, Culture, Multilingualism, and Youth (2012). School autonomy is more effective the more it is accompanied by the context in which more fair and measurable tools for assessing school performance are used (e.g., external examinations); adequate mechanisms for ensuring quality in education are provided; special measurement tools are used in schools located in underprivileged environments; and finally, the role, responsibility, and competencies of the leaders or principals are clearly defined.

The Eurydice report (2013) showed that systems in which schools have more autonomy tend to more frequently and successfully introduce new solutions in the field of delegating or distributing leadership (this is what the governments of Finland and the Netherlands have done).

In Poland, the vast majority of reports devoted to school leadership have the head of the school as the main "hero." Much less attention is devoted to teachers who are or may be informal school leaders in introducing instructional, character education, and other innovations leading to the improved effectiveness of the school. Effectiveness was understood not only as achieving better teaching results by students but also as better school climate and genuine bonds with parents, the local community, and school graduates.

There are also studies focusing on human resources management, finances, gaining sponsors, and partners with whom cooperation may be beneficial for the school. In all these cases, the assessment is primarily the administrative work of the principal.

In Poland, the selection for the teaching profession is not always too demanding. It is rather formal, and only one candidate enters competition for the post of school principal. Unfortunately, there are also cases where the competition itself is a mere formality, and the candidate has already been selected by properly picked members of the competition commission.

As mentioned before, it is worth emphasizing that the lack of candidates for the post of principal is also common in other European countries. It seems that these deficiencies in selecting school leaders will diminish if the prestige of the teaching profession increases. It is interesting that teachers themselves assess the teaching profession much lower than the general public. To some extent, this translates into the attitudes of principals as almost all Polish principals are recruited from teachers.

In some opinions on school leadership, one can also see more evidence regarding the division of leader's responsibilities. Traditionally, the school is no longer managed by only one person, the principal, but leadership at school can be, and is, shared by many people (Pont, Nusche, & Moorman, 2008). "Decentralized" leadership consists in joint decision-making and managing the school in a way that allows for an increased role of students and school employees. Such a shift toward the division of leadership may be useful for other reasons as well. There are more organizational changes resulting in the flattening of management structures, increasing school autonomy.

In addition, distributed leadership can be more effective in facing the challenges of an increasingly complex, information-rich society (Pont et al., 2008). Such an approach does not have to diminish the role of the principal, who is central in leading the teachers in the process of "division of power." Single and shared leadership can exist with one common goal: to support the process of teaching children and youth.

However, the Eurydice report (2013) on teachers and school principals in Europe indicated that the practice differs from theoretical assumptions. According to this source, in most countries, school leadership managing the school was limited to formal teams or management groups. Most often, this means that one or several deputy principals and sometimes an administrative assistant or an accountant supports the head. The insufficient role of management in introducing educational innovations, new pedagogical approaches, and creative use of technology, including information and computer-related techniques, was also noted (Euridice, 2013).

This was somewhat different in the context of Polish education law, especially in the situation of deepening tensions between local government authorities and the school environment, represented mostly by teachers' trade unions. The legislator delegated a number of employer rights indirectly and directly to the school governing authorities, such as communes, municipalities, and city districts, and therefore predominantly to local self-government units. In practice, the principal is often the manager who is tasked with organizing the work of subordinates but is not always independent even in personnel matters (Więsław, 2011). Thus, on the one hand, the role of principals is undermined. It is difficult to consider this as a division of the management process.

On the other hand, many people think that in Poland, the classic style of leadership prevails, the style consisting in the dominant position of the principal or a narrow group of people associated with him/her. Official orders are often issued without explaining the purpose of the action.

The literature on the subject of leadership is growing rapidly. New concepts appear and the old ones are presented in new contexts. Researchers are trying to capture the diverse face of leadership; on the one hand, practices focused on pedagogical activities, and on the other, individualistic versus collectivist character of leadership practices.

The synthetic and subjective context of determinants for the school head's functioning (far less frequently a school leader who is not necessarily a principal) emphasizes some of the political nature related to the practice of teaching and performing the function of a principal. National and cultural contexts often play their part as well.

THE SCHOOL PRINCIPAL IN LIGHT OF SELECTED STUDIES

This part of the text presents the results of selected research on school leadership understood primarily as a way of conduct, and attitudes of school principals. There are large quantitative surveys conducted on an international scale, as well as in-depth qualitative case studies.

The Teaching and Learning International Survey (TALIS) studies (OECD 2009, 2013) were addressed to teachers and school principals. In 2008, the study covered twenty-four countries with over 90,000 teachers and several thousand school principals. The participants were in equivalent to the Polish lower secondary school, grades 7–9. In 2013, 172,000 teachers and over 10,000 principals from 33 countries participated in the study. The study was extended to all school levels, although it was not obligatory and in most countries was carried out in grades 7–9 (in Poland in primary, lower secondary, and upper secondary schools).

In addition to the issues related to teachers, including sociodemographic characteristics of the teachers, their professional development, the conditions in which they worked, and attitudes and beliefs concerning teaching and pedagogical practices, school leadership was an important part of this study.

Assuming that school leadership plays an important role in strengthening effective teaching and the environment in which the process of gaining knowledge by students takes place, TALIS 2008 and 2013 described the role of school leaders and explored the support they provide to their teachers. Exploring these and other issues not mentioned earlier had one common goal, to increase the scope of available international information for Organisation for Economic Co-operation and Development countries and other stakeholders regarding teachers, teaching, and indirectly, the impact teachers can have on students' learning. The evidence for this is provided by fairly large literature on the subject and the findings of other studies (Pont et al., 2008).

Administrative support for the teachers can be found within four dimensions, including building a school vision, developing particular goals and priorities, offering individual support, and developing school collaboration culture. These four have proven to be a significant predictor of job satisfaction and teacher willingness to stay in the profession (Tickle, Chang, & Kim, 2011 as cited in OECD 2013). This support from school principals also turned out to be effective in other matters, such as mediation regarding teacher's wages and the influence of pupils' behavior on the level of job satisfaction (Tickle et al., 2011).

These are sufficient reasons to take a closer look at the following issues: the characteristics of school leaders and school leadership; how leadership styles are related to the management of teaching staff, their professional development, practices, and beliefs, as well as teacher appraisal and the feedback based on the appraisal (teachers should be not only assessed but also informed about the most important conclusions resulting from this assessment).

Traditionally, principals have a key position in management and leadership at the school level. More broadly, this leadership consists of two key descriptors, instructional and administrative leadership styles. As TALIS 2008 study showed, most principals represent both styles at the same time. It is worth adding here that Polish principals taking part in this study clearly demonstrated more often the instructional rather than administrative style (Piwowarski & Krawczyk, 2009). This style of leadership is primarily focused on improving learning outcomes achieved by students.

Such principals support the development of teacher subject teams, appraise teachers and inform them about the conclusions of this appraisal, model effective curricula, and support the analysis of student achievement data at class level (Blase & Blasé, 2000 as cited in OECD, 2013). The TALIS study (2008) findings have also shown that in schools where the instructional leadership style prevailed, the principals were more likely to target teachers with weaker results offering help in the form of various types of professional development, eliminating these weaknesses (TALIS 2009, p. 204).

In addition to the previously mentioned leadership styles that were identified in the TALIS study (2008), which were comparable to findings in the source literature, five scales of school management behaviors were identified. The first three were: (1) management of school goals; (2) instructional management; and (3) direct supervision of instruction. On each of them, the Polish lower secondary schools' directors occupied a place well above the average calculated on the basis of data from all the countries participating in the survey.

Management of School Goals

High scores on this scale meant that the principals defined the school's goals by frequently using the results of exams and other measures of students' school achievements and adjusted the curriculum, class schedule, and professional development of teachers in their school to attain these goals.

Instructional Management

Principals often worked with teachers to overcome their weaknesses together and solve particular instructional problems. They often informed their teachers about the possibilities of updating knowledge and raising qualifications. This group of principals also paid attention to the disruptive behavior of students. They devoted a lot of time to work on the teaching practice of particular teachers.

Direct Supervision of Instruction

Principals often observed instruction in classrooms and offered suggestions on how teachers could improve their teaching skills and often monitored students' work (Piwowarski & Krawczyk, 2009).

The three scales of management methods constituted *an instruction-oriented leadership style*. As mentioned earlier, Polish principals of lower secondary schools predominantly used this type of leadership style.

The other two scales were: (1) accountable management; and (2) bureaucratic management, understood as procedure oriented, without the pejorative overtone.

Accountable Management

High scores on this scale meant that principals felt responsible to the education authorities, parents, and other external school partners. They ensured that ministerial teaching recommendations were explained to new teachers and that these recommendations were applied by all teachers. These principals also believed that presenting, in a convincing way, new ideas concerning the school's functioning to parents was an important element of their work.

Bureaucratic Management

Principals with high scores on bureaucratic management believed that it was important for the school to ensure that everyone followed the same set of rules. They considered creating an atmosphere of order and discipline in school as an important element of their work.

The scores of Polish principals on these two scales were lower than the average calculated for the countries participating in the study. Based on both scores, the principals and states were assigned to the group in which the *administrative leadership style* prevailed (OECD, 2009; Piwowarski & Krawczyk, 2009).

The TALIS study (2013) re-examined the importance of school leadership. Some indicators regarding the characteristics of schools and principals were reused. Similar to the previous study, the age, gender, professional experience, and education of principals were considered, allowing comparison of how these factors corresponded to the styles of management and the conditions of environments in which teaching and learning took place. It is worth emphasizing that the school leadership (somewhat unexpectedly for the project management) obtained the highest priority among the countries participating in the TALIS 2013 survey; more precisely, this was found to be true among countries that participated in a special vote before implementation of the project (twenty-five countries, among them Poland). Each country had at its disposal 200 points, which could be freely assigned to twenty proposed topics. School leadership received the most points, with 393, followed by teacher beliefs and practice with 374 points. In last place, with 86 points, were issues concerning the effectiveness of student admission to schools. Naturally, this issue was not included in the study in 2013.

These and other studies (Pont et al., 2008) indicate that the instructional management style is more beneficial and effective for the students' and school's outcomes. The TALIS study (2008) results showed that in schools where instructional management style prevails, teachers cooperated more often and had a higher sense of job satisfaction.

In the TALIS study (2008), no correlations were identified between school goals and styles represented by school principals (showed in the figure earlier) and instructional practices used by teachers during classes, the level of school autonomy, or the form of school ownership (public or private). However, from the point of view of the principals themselves, it is not so obvious how to manage the school. There were many who felt the need to improve, broaden their knowledge in the fields of management, law, and sometimes even construction law.

At the OSKKO congress (Ogólnopolskie Stowarzyszenie Kadry Kierowniczej Oświaty—National Association of Education Management Staff) in Toruń, Poland, in September 2012, the scope of predispositions, knowledge, and skills of school principals was discussed. Questions were asked whether the principal should be a teacher or a manager, and if one can be a school principal without having been a teacher. Some of these questions were answered by the TALIS 2013 survey (the aforementioned issues were introduced at the national level, referring only to Poland).

In the light of the TALIS study (2013) findings, similar to the other countries surveyed, a typical principal in Poland was about fifty years old. Almost half of the Polish principals were aged 50–59 and were least frequently recruited from persons under the age of forty (64 percent). There were noticeable differences between individual countries, for example, in Romania, about 31 percent of lower secondary school teachers were less than forty years old, and in Italy, almost half were over sixty. Considering the age of principals, when comparing data collected in 2013 with the data from 2008, there was some stability among staff occupying this position.

During the five years in Poland, the percentage of principals in the younger age groups decreased by 20 percentage points, with the highest decrease in the 40–49 age group at 14 percentage points. The proportion of people aged 50–59 increased (Hernik, 2015).

In Poland, the majority of school principals were women. This situation diverged from the international average, where women are the majority among teachers but not among the principals. Poland is the fourth of the 34 countries surveyed in terms of the proportion of women school principals. At the same time, it is worth noting that the higher the school level, the numerical superiority of women among principals decreased and the chances of becoming a principal for male teachers are much higher than those of female teachers.

The averages calculated for the principals from all countries participating in the survey indicate that, especially in primary schools, these chances are more than twice as high, in upper secondary schools 1.9, and in lower secondary schools 1.5. Comparing these ratios with other countries taking part in the survey, female teachers of Polish lower secondary schools in comparison with those of other European countries still had the greatest chances of becoming a principal, after Norway (1.1) and Romania (1.3). In some countries, women's chances of assuming the position of a school principal were very low (i.e., in Korea, men's chances were 14 times higher than women's, in Japan 10 times higher, while in Europe the lowest chances were observed in Portugal (4.2), Estonia (3.8), and Finland (3.6) (Hernik, 2015, pp. 73–74).

Cultural considerations may play an important part in this case. Various studies show that a large part of Polish society is still in favor of the traditional division of roles and spheres of activity for males and females (Siemieńska, 2000). Women are, as it were, self-limiting and reluctant to undertake typically masculine tasks, and the principal's position may be perceived as such.

Various studies show that a large part of Polish society is still in favor of the traditional division of roles and spheres of activity for males and females (Siemieńska, 2000). Interestingly, it turns out that holding the post of a kindergarten principal does not fall within this logic. It does not seem "masculine" or prestigious enough, as this role was held by women only, and local governments report problems finding people willing to take this position (Herczyński & Sobotka, 2012).

The TALIS study (2013) attempted to capture the existence of a culture of cooperation between management, teachers, and parents in making decisions at school. To this end, a *distributed leadership* scale was created, and linear regression analyses were conducted to show its possible relationships with other factors. At the international level, few consistent and statistically significant relationships have been found between the distributed leadership scale and other variables, that is, the characteristics of the school or principal.

It could be noted, however, that principals scoring high on the scale of distributed leadership more frequently worked in schools that were characterized by an atmosphere of mutual support and openness between staff (in twenty-three countries, including Poland), and were more satisfied with their work (in seventeen countries, also in Poland).

Another construct that was explored in the TALIS study (2013), similar to 2008, was *instructional leadership*. The linear regression analyses indicated that principals scoring high on the instructional leadership scale more often declared that they

- used student results to define school goals and develop educational programs (in twelve countries);
- worked on a professional development plan for their school (in nineteen countries);
- spent more time on tasks related to the curriculum and teaching practice (in seven countries);
- conducted direct observation of the lessons as part of the formal appraisal of teachers (in twenty-four countries, including Poland);
- developed a professional development or training plan following a teacher appraisal (in fifteen countries, including Poland);
- imposed material sanctions on teacher, such as a reduction in the annual salary increase, if the teacher's performance was considered unsatisfactory (in seventeen countries);
- increased the probability of his or her promotion following the teacher's appraisal (in fifteen countries); and
- worked in schools in which there was a positive school climate, characterized by mutual support (in fifteen countries) (Hernik, 2015, pp. 87–88).

Depending on the school level, from 84 percent to 95 percent of Polish principals reported that they used student results, including national and international surveys, to define educational goals and programs for the school, and almost all (96 percent) were working on a professional development plan for the school. Interestingly, the principals of Finnish lower secondary schools whose students are known worldwide as achieving high scores in the Programme for International Student Assessment (PISA) study paid less attention to the student results than those managing schools in other countries (74 percent of Finnish principals).

Additionally, in the analyses, correlations were identified between the instructional leadership and other variables, but the vectors of these relationships were not consistent among all participating countries. It is worth the instructional leadership and other variables, but the vectors of noting, however, that in Poland principals achieving high scores on the scale of instructional leadership more often reported that following the teacher's appraisal, a mentor was appointed to help him or her improve the teaching methods, the teacher's professional responsibilities changed, including the number of teaching hours, administrative duties, and the contract with the teacher was either not renewed or the teacher was dismissed.

In the majority of TALIS study participating countries, both leadership scales were correlated. Principals who concentrated in their activities mainly on the implementation of instructional goals tended to simultaneously ensure that other employees are involved in the school management process. However, this was not the case in Poland, where both scales were not correlated. Polish principals gave very similar responses on the distributed leadership scale, resulting in small variance of scores, which resulted in low correlation values.

A slightly different approach to the study of management styles in the TALIS study (2013) resulted in the dissolution of clear differences in management styles among Polish principals, regardless of the type of school (in the 2008 study, a clear instructional style and dominance was observed). About two-thirds of the respondents did not have a dominant style, less than one-third had a dominant instructional style, and a small percentage only endorsed distributed management style (2 percent). However, there were statistically significant differences in leadership styles depending on the respondent's gender. For females, identification of a particular management style was clearer; in the case of instructional leadership, it did not depend on the type of school, and in the case of distributed leadership, it was observed in primary school principals (Hernik, 2015).

Due to the fact that in many studies, the theme of *school autonomy and principal's work* appears to be important for the effective management of an educational institution, it is worth presenting some of the results of TALIS studies (2008, 2013).

School autonomy was examined in the TALIS study (2008) on the basis of information gathered from school principals. The analysis covered thirteen areas of decisions made at the school level, where the principal, teachers, or the school-managing board were responsible for making the decisions:

> (1) selecting teachers for hire; (2) dismissing teachers; (3) establishing teachers' starting salary; (4) determining teachers' salary increases; (5) allocation of funds for teachers' professional development; (6) formulating the school budget; (7) deciding on budget allocations within the school; (8) establishing student disciplinary policies; (9) establishing student assessment policies; (10) approving students for admission to the school; (11) deciding which courses are offered; (12) determining courses content; and (13) choosing which textbooks are used.
> (OECD, 2009, p. 36)

While analyzing these areas, and taking into account all the teachers surveyed in twenty-four countries, it can be concluded that the responsibility of school principals, and hence autonomy, was the greatest in the area of: establishing student disciplinary policies (95 percent of teachers worked in schools whose principals indicated that the process of establishing the policy takes place at the school level; for Poland, it was 100 percent), choosing which textbooks are used (90 percent of overall respondents; Polish responses indicated 99.5 percent), and establishing student assessment policies (88.9 percent overall; Polish respondents indicated 97.3 percent).

The principals had the least influence in setting the starting salary (24.3 percent overall; responses from Poland 43.2 percent) and salary increases (25.6 percent overall; Poland, 48.2 percent; Piwowarski & Krawczyk, 2009, p. 16). The above indicators and those concerning hiring and dismissal of teachers were very diverse. The latter, on average, for all teachers from the countries participating in the survey, assumed much higher values: more than 60 percent of principals were responsible for decisions in those areas. However, the value of salary-related and hiring/dismissal indicators in individual countries ranged from a few dozen to 90 percent–100 percent (OECD 2009, Table 2.7, p. 44).

There were countries, including Poland, in which 100 percent occurred many times in individual areas of autonomy, indicating a large degree of school autonomy. This manifests itself in the responsibility and autonomy of the principal's work. One can distinguish a research approach deviating methodologically from the results presented earlier, and which is worth noting, exploring the role of school principals in environments that are underprivileged or disadvantaged in some respect.

For example, these may include areas where, in the early 1990s, large state farms were decommissioned in Poland and in which a characteristic subculture of professional inactivity emerged, or districts inhabited by ethnic minorities, or surrounding closed factories in large American cities or Western Europe. These latter environments are of interest to researchers from the point of view of the traits exhibited or suppressed by school principals. The phenomenon observed in the United States, where results achieved by students are generally lower in highly urbanized areas or large cities, is not yet visible on a massive scale in Poland; rather, the reverse is true.

It is also worth noting that considering the subject of the study, "going deeper" into the given issues can be carried out on a much smaller scale and using qualitative research methodology. This was not the method used in the TALIS surveys; in 2013, over 10,000 school principals took part. In a case study involving three American schools, principals, teachers, and student results were examined. The incentive for the study was the fact that the schools were operating in a very poor urban environment, but their students' results had been above the high results in the region for five consecutive years (Litchka, 2011). The questions were: What were the principals of these schools like; and what personal qualities did they have that made their students /and/or schools more than a one-off success?

It is known that the work of principals in such schools is more difficult, the schools have less resources than those operating in much richer suburbs. Expectations of students are also much lower. Despite these obstacles, there have been principals who were successful in such difficult learning environments.

To study the leadership skills, the *Leadership Practices Inventory* (Kouzes & Posner, 2001) was used, which had already been used in over 100 educational studies (Litchka, 2011) and, as the authors of the instrument declared, has been used by over three million people from many disciplines, not only education. According to Kouzes and Posner (2003), the leadership practices inventory measures five practices used by leaders: (1) model the way; (2) inspire a shared vision; (3) challenge the process; (4) enable others to act; and (5) encourage the heart.

Litchka (2011) found that the most significant trait of principals influencing the success of students and the school, both in their self-assessment and in the opinion of teachers, was having a vision of leadership or visionary leadership. Similar conclusions were found in a comparative study on effective leadership in socially disadvantaged areas focused in Łódź, Poland, and Sheffield, England.

In addition, Madalińska-Michalak (2012) found that the properly fulfilled role of the school's principal was a precondition for accelerating the change in school, contributing to enhancing educational opportunities for young people in socially disadvantaged areas, and having a vision of school development was an important measure of the effectiveness of principal's work.

At the beginning of 2013, a joint comparative study of school leadership in the United States and in Poland began, led by Professor Peter Litchka of Loyola University Maryland, United States, and Professor Rafał Piwowarski of the University of Białystok, in Białystok, Poland. The trial study included 112 principals in Poland and 179 principals in the United States, participants coming from various environments and schools at all levels of education. This study was wider than the ones concerning disadvantaged environments mentioned earlier.

The initial results indicated that the American principals in their self-assessment obtained higher results than their Polish counterparts in every leadership practice (Kouzes and Posner, 2003). In addition, the Polish results were more diversified as evidenced by the values of standard deviations, calculated for each average value of leadership practice.

Tentatively, it can be pointed out that for the American principals, the two most significant leadership practices influencing their students' and school's success were setting a personal example and designating the direction of actions and encouraging others to act. Polish principals reported that it was important to honestly and warmly appreciate the staff and enable people to act. Therefore, there were some differences and similarities between principal's practices. If these were confirmed in other comparative studies, researchers should look to answer two questions: if there are some common traits of the people who effectively perform the function of the school head; and if so, to what are the differences attributed.

These studies also indicated that principals assess their leadership practices differently than their teachers (generally teachers much more negatively) (Litchka, 2011; Piwowarski 2014). Further research should explore when, in what situations, and why these differences are more or less significant. These are just a few of the questions the answers to which can satisfy the curiosity of the researchers, as well as tell practitioners and educational authorities what leadership traits principals, or those aspiring to be, should exhibit or develop.

Many studies and research findings also point to the role of school leadership in building the right school climate (TALIS citations). Most of the charters of Polish schools contain passages making the principal responsible for creating the right atmosphere of work based on the principles of kindness and mutual respect. The principal's orientation toward working with the school's social environment and with the students' parents also plays an important part.

Maintaining close relations with local institutions results in a better embedding of the school in the local community, which is much easier in small towns. Smaller number of inhabitants created stronger informal bonds between members of the community, as well as greater social control. Less often, but also in large cities, there are examples of close cooperation between leaders and the local environment, thanks to the leaders' clear vision of the school's functioning (Współpraca szkół [Cooperation between Schools], 2012).

RECOMMENDATIONS REGARDING THE PRINCIPAL

A unique decalogue (ten statements) regarding effective school leadership was formulated by Day (Day, 2007; Day & Leithwood, 2014). It delivered a clear and well-argued message for trainers of school principal sand creators of educational policy. It argued for preparing principals to initiate and manage changes so that the right conditions for the development of principals are created. In Day's (DATE) opinion, however, the main traits of effective school principals around the world should be courage, commitment, trust, empathy, and perseverance.

Hernik (2015) believed that in Poland, it is necessary to shift the system of training principals toward educational leadership. This system should:

- include diverse elements—on the one hand, it should include leadership competences and the ability to efficiently raise additional funds. On the other hand, this system should also give principals a sense of direction in the complex legal system in which the school functions.
- include the elements of practical training, for example, in the positions of the school's vice-heads or outside the education system and also preparing in training schools.
- include the period before and during employment, so that responding to emerging difficulties and needs was possible on an ongoing basis. In the current legal system, there are no formal requirements for the professional development of the principal.
- include support and cooperation networks for principals, especially at the local level.

The principal's responsibilities would have to be reduced and some transferred to other entities, such as the school council, teachers' council, or students' parents. This would require introducing changes, including in the teachers' professional promotion system, breaking promotions away from a strictly financial function and introducing a newly defined two-track promotion system, horizontal and vertical.

In the first case, a horizontal promotion could be about creating positions related to carrying out some tasks and playing a number of roles concerning different areas of the school's functioning in addition to teaching in the classroom, for example, position of a mentor, school mediator, school project coordinator, fundraiser, or school-parents cooperation facilitator. Teachers' involvement in carrying out tasks of this type should include reducing the basic teaching load, as well as some form of financial compensation. On the other hand, the vertical promotion should be associated with greater responsibility and could include a team leader or a professional development manager position.

Devolving some of the tasks to parents requires a change in the approach to this issue. First, it would require the departure from formalistic and bureaucratic treatment of the parents' council as a "producer of consent" on all documents and give it a greater freedom for making decisions.

Second, it would require developing more channels of communication with parents in addition to parents' councils. It relieves the school head of some tasks, gives parents more space to engage, and allows for making use of parents' energy, activity, and talents, which in the current formula of cooperation has no chance to emerge and remain unused (Hernik, 2015). This approach may be too idealistic, especially in relation to the passive attitude of the majority of parents, but certainly should be attempted.

SUMMARY

School leadership is a complex and multidimensional category. There are many definitions and research approaches of which only a small portion has been presented. The presentation of transformational, transactional, or systemic leadership was not undertaken, and distributed leadership was only mentioned. Sometimes theoretical approaches diverge from reality, which cannot always be encapsulated in a strict, normative formula. It is not always possible to perfectly link theory with current education policy, which is why some experts point to the fact that research projects and comparative studies concerning good leadership practices are not always feasible in real-life situations. There is no single leadership model that could be easily introduced in different schools and at different levels of teaching. The research findings tend to support the thesis that the principal is more the manager of a company than the leader who does not forget who the main beneficiary of the school is.

From the TALIS survey (2013), an image of Polish principals emerges as persons who, on one hand, are overloaded with their duties without sufficient support and commitment on the part of parents and who are struggling with insufficient budget and other school resources; on the other hand, they are also persons who take on more and more tasks without sharing responsibility with others. There is a visible tension between the desire to maintain control wherever possible and the inability to deal with it, leading to problems in focusing on leadership activities.

The findings of the TALIS study (2009, 2013) support the view that the system of training for the position of a school principal requires thorough changes aimed at shaping the educational leader. Managers of Polish schools have definitely shorter-than-international average professional experience in managerial positions both in and outside of school. Therefore, school principal positions are taken by people without previous practical experience in the field of management.

The TALIS data (2013) showed that Polish principals were generally well prepared for their work, in that they had completed qualification courses and training related to school administration but were relatively poorly trained in educational leadership. Then there was also the problem of the lack of appropriate solutions for the professional development of principals. As teachers, they needed to develop professionally, but there was no adequate offer for them; further, the costs of participation in such activities were too high and the training was incompatible with their work plan.

Research projects increasingly provide knowledge to educational authorities, policy makers. Whatever has up till now been limited to small and closed circulation, scientific exchange in research environments—breaks into the highest level of education policy, which initiates increasingly surveys, projects. Perhaps, this is partly a "window dressing game" on the part of the world of politics, bureaucratic treatments of powerful international institutions and political groups, and to a lesser extent the action of individual governments.

However, regardless of how quickly and to what an extent this knowledge will serve to achieve more effective education, these initiatives should be assessed positively. It should also be remembered that researchers, and academics, in creating knowledge and organizing it in the form of theory, have other goals than education policy makers. Policy makers are focused on lowering huge public education outlays or achieving better results.

Researchers and academics are sometimes too distracted from reality, while paradoxically, policy makers may know more, because they can take advantage of much more generous funding and it is easier for them to raise the money for research. Therefore, it is necessary to accept this situation and share roles. The scientific community provides expertise and methodological knowledge, while politicians provide financial and organizational support to projects, they regard as a priority.

REFERENCES

Blase, J., & Blasé, J. (2000). Effective instructional leadership: Teachers' perspectives on how principals promote teaching and learning in schools. *Journal of Educational Administration, 38*(2), 130–141.

Council of the European Union (2013). *Leadership in education: Discussion paper* (2013, July 9). Brussels, Belgium: Council of the European Union.

Day, C. (2014). Budowanie i podtrzymywanie sukcesu w przywództwie szkolnym (Building and sustaining success in school leadership (translated by. J. Madalińska-Michalak). In: Kwiatkowski, S. M., & Madalińska-Michalak, J. (Eds.), *Przywództwo edukacyjne. Współczesne wyzwania* (*Educational leadership: Contemporary challenge*). Warszawa: ABC a Wolter Kluwer business, 119–154.

Day, C., & Leithwood, K. (2007). *Successful principalship leadership in times of change: International perspectives*. Dordrecht, Netherlands: Springer Science+Business Media.

Dorczak, R. (2013). Dyrektor szkoły jako przywódca edukacyjny—próba określenia kompetencji kluczowych. (Principal as an educational leader: An Attempt to determine key competences). W: Mazurkiewicz, G. (red), *Przywództwo i zmiana w edukacji. Edukacja jako mechanizm doskonalenia.* (In: Mazurkiewicz, G. (Ed.), *Leadership and change in education. Education as a mechanism for improvement.*) Kraków: Wydawnictwo Uniwersytetu Jagiellońskiego, 75–88.

European Commission, Communication from the Commission. (2012). Rethinking education: Investing in skills for better socio-economic outcomes. *Communication from the Commission*. Retrieved from https://ec.europa.eu/

europeaid/rethinking-education-investing-skills-better-socio-economic-outcomes-com2012-669_enEACEA/Eurydice.

(2013). *Key data on teachers and school leaders in Europe, 2013 edition*. Euridice Report. Eurydice: Publication Office of the European Union. Retrieved from https://publications.europa.eu/en/publication-detail.

Herczyński, J., & Sobotka, A. (2012). Dyskusje o pozycji zawodowej dyrektora szkoły (Discussions about the status of the headmaster). In: M. Herbst (Ed.), *Decentralizacja oświaty (Decentralisation of education)*.Warsaw, Poland: ICM UW, and available from URL: www.ore.edu.pl.

Hernik, K. (Ed.). (2015). *Polscy nauczyciele i dyrektorzy w Międzynarodowym Badaniu Nauczania i Uczenia się TALIS 2013 (Polish teachers and directors in the International Teaching Research and Learning TALIS 2013)*. Warsaw, Poland: Institute for Educational Research, and available from URL: www.eduentuzjasci.pl.

Hernik, K., Wasilewska, O., & Kasprzak, T. (2012). Kierunki rozwoju przywództwa szkolnego w Europie (Directions of development of school leadership in Europe). *Polityka Społeczna (Social Policy), 1*, 10–15.

Kouzes, J., & Posner, B. (2001). *Leadership practices inventory*. San Francisco, CA: Jossey-Bass.

Kouzes, J., & Posner, B. (2003). *The five practices of exemplary leaders*. San Francisco, CA: Pfeiffer.

Litchka, P. (2011). The leadership abilities of a principle in a high achieving, high poverty urban school. *Edukacja (Education), 3*, 42–50.

Madalińska-Michalak, J. (2012). *Skuteczne przywództwo w szkołach na obszarach zaniedbanych społecznie. Studium porównawcze (Effective leadership in schools in socially neglected areas: Comparative study)*. Łódź, Poland: University of Łódź.

Organisation for Economic Co-operation and Development. (2009). *Creating effective teaching and learning environments: First results from TALIS*. Paris, France: OECD.

Organisation for Economic Co-operation and Development. (2013, June). *Teaching and Learning International Survey: TALIS 2013, conceptual framework*. Paris, France: OECD.

Organisation for Economic Co-operation and Development. (2014a). *TALIS 2013 result: An international perspective on teaching and learning*. Paris, France: OECD.

Organisation for Economic Co-operation and Development. (2014b). *TALIS 2013: Technical report*. Paris, France: OECD.

Piwowarski, R. (2014). Wybrane strategie badania przywództwa szkolnego (Selected strategies for studying school leadership). *Ruch Pedagogiczny (Pedagogical Movement), 1*, 97–107.

Piwowarski, R., & Krawczyk, M. (2009). *TALIS. Nauczanie—Wyniki Badań 2008. Polska na tle międzynarodowym.(TALIS. Teaching—Research results 2008. Poland on the international background)*. Warsaw, Poland: Ministry of National Education, Institute for Educational Research, and available from URL: www. eduentuzjasci.edu.pl.

Pont, B., Nusche, D., & H. Moorman. (Eds.). (2008). *Improving school leadership: Case studies on system leadership* (Vol. 2). Paris, France: OECD.

Siemieńska, R. (2000). *Nie mogą, nie chcą czy nie potrafią? O postawach i uczestnictwie politycznym kobiet w Polsce (They can not, do not want or can not? On the attitudes and political participation of women in Poland)*. Warsaw, Poland: Scholar.

Tickle, B. R., Chang, M., & Kim, S. (2011). Administrative support and its mediating effect on U.S. public school teachers, *Teaching and Teacher Education, 27*(2), 342–349.

Więsław, S.(2011). *Situation and professional status of school directors and educational institutions*. Warsaw, Poland: Center for Education Development.

Współpraca szkół z podmiotami zewnętrznymi. Raport z badania otoczenia instytucjonalnego przedszkoli, szkół podstawowych i gimnazjów (Cooperation between schools and external entities. Report on the institutional environment of kindergartens, primary and junior high schools). (2012). Warsaw, Poland: Institute for Educational Research.

Chapter Two

The Australian Education Revolution

The Impact of a Reform Movement on School Leadership and System Performance

Jack Rice

Justin Garrick

The Australian Education Revolution (Ministers Media Center, 2008) took place from 2008 to 2013 under the direction of Australian Labor Party. It is an important case study that highlights the effects of a national education reform strategy on a country's education system. Considering the quantum of investment, the short time frame to implementation, and the pervasiveness of the reform elements, the Australian Education Revolution may be unprecedented in its scope. A thorough analysis of the time period, its prelude, intentions, and consequences may serve as a cautionary tale as worldwide governments grapple with system-wide education reforms. While the Education Revolution's intended outcomes went unfulfilled in the short term, the issues raised and competencies developed during the period will continue to constructively inform Australia's national conversations on education well into the future.

THE HISTORY AND ORGANIZATION OF EDUCATION IN AUSTRALIA

The first British colony was founded in Australia in 1788 in an area known as New South Wales (Tourism Australia, 2018). Over the next 100 years, a loose system of elementary schools slowly developed in Australia's fledgling colonies. Today, the Australian Federation consists of six states (New South Wales, Queensland, Victoria, Tasmania, South Australia, and Western Australia) and two territories (Northern Territory and the Australian Capital Territory).

Australia is the sixth-largest country in the world by land mass but contains a population of only 24 million (Nationmaster, 2018). The bulk of the population can be found in five major urban centers. As a consequence of its geography, education in Australia deals with issues stemming from rural versus urban divides and the impact of remoteness. For example, rural and remote schools in Australia are statistically more likely to serve lower socioeconomic status (SES) cohorts of students. These jurisdictions struggle for resources, including experienced teachers (Lamb, Jackson, Walstab, & Huo, 2015).

Prior to 1964, Australia consisted of government schools, which were funded by states and territories, and nongovernment schools (mostly Catholic) that were funded privately. The federal government did not fund schools directly. Consequently, there was no mechanism by which the commonwealth government could directly impact schools.

Then, in the following decade, a series of events changed the landscape of federal government participation into the education space. These events involved capital funding for government and nongovernment schools, recurrent funding for nongovernment schools, and finally, the extension of federal funding to government schools through the Australian Schools Commission. Each of these actions had political motivations but their cumulative effect created an ability for the Australian federal government to flex its muscle by using educational funding as its lever.

INCREASING FEDERAL PARTICIPATION IN EDUCATION

In 1962, Bishop Cullinane of Canberra and Goulburn temporarily closed the Catholic Independent Schools, which were under his supervision, citing a lack of operational funds (Devine, 1991). Hence, 2,000 Catholic students would be displaced to six government schools, which could not accommodate the overflow. A temporary compromise was reached by the distribution of emergency state aid to the Catholic education office. This conflict produced a chasm between the Catholic Church and the opposition Labor Party with which it had historically been aligned but were in opposition on the issue of the funding of Independent Schools. Prime Minister Robert Menzies and the Liberal government seized the opportunity and adopted state aid for nongovernment schools (Independent and Catholic) as a campaign issue. Menzies won the 1963 election in a landslide, and this proved that supporting nongovernment schools was an acceptable political strategy.

Continuing their venture into educational policy and pointing to a perceived desperate need to improve Australian schooling, the Australian Commonwealth Government also began capital grants to government and nongovernment schools in 1964. Initially only for science laboratories and equipment for secondary schools, the program was expanded to include libraries five years later and rose from an initial payout of $5M AUD to a schedule, which exceeded $20M AUD by 1970 (Harrington, 2011).

This was the first substantive foray by the Australian Commonwealth into the education system, and it proved to be a popular mechanism to influence the direction of educational policy as Menzies was re-elected as part of a coalition government with very little opposition raised to the capital grants scheme. The awarding of federal capital funding to both government and nongovernment schools still exists in Australia today, through the provision of a number of different capital grant programs. This act is crucial in understanding today's Australian Education context, as it was the first time that nongovernment schools were allowed to participate in public funding. There would be no going back.

Buoyed by Father Cullinane's successful stance, archdioceses around Australia continued to put pressure on the government to support Independent and Catholic schools. In 1970, recurrent per student grants for nongovernment schools were formally introduced. The first independent school subsidies to nongovernment schools were set at $35 per primary student and $50 per secondary student. From 1973, these grants were to be fixed at a rate equivalent to 20 percent of the cost of educating a child in a government school (Bennett, 2008). Cullinane's gambit to increase public funding for Catholic schools was successful, but it had lasting implications as non-Catholic independent schools now qualified for government funding leading to an overall expansion of Independent education in the country.

Following the guidelines of the Karmel Report (Karmel, 1973), one of the most important acts introduced by the Australian federal government was the *Schools Commission Act of 1973, as the new Labor government, led by Gough Whitlam, would attempt to influence education in the country (Cumming & Mawdsley, 2012). However instead of reverting back to the Labor party's celebrated platform of non-support for Independent schools, the Whitlam administration left intact recurrent funding for independent schools and extended the recurrent funding arrangement to include government schools. From this point forward, the Commonwealth government would no longer be a spectator in education. With this act, all schools in Australia, both government and nongovernment, would receive recurrent federal funding. In conjunction with previous agreements, they would also be eligible for capital grants programs.*

Despite these subtle intrusions, in the time period between 1973 and 2008, the Australian Commonwealth government played an important, but overall benign, role in education. It allowed the various colleges of teachers within its states to drive educational policies and articulate their own outcomes. The federal government monitored benchmark standards, but for the most part simply operated as a bank for both government and nongovernment schools.

There was no doubt that due to these fluctuations in funding policies, the composition of Australian education was changing. In 1970, 20 percent of students attended nongovernment schools, either Catholic or Independent; by 2010, 35 percent of students attended nongovernment schools. Today over 40 percent of all Australian secondary students attend a nongovernment school. This far outweighs the average of Organisation for Economic Co-operation and Development (OECD) countries (18 percent) and eclipses the proportions in the United States (8 percent) and Canada (6 percent) (Rowe, 2017).

As families began to choose nongovernment schools and the landscape of Australian education began to change, questions of system performance, accountability, and national competitiveness began to emerge. In 2008, the Commonwealth would use these issues as a policy platform to substantially reform Australian education.

THE MELBOURNE DECLARATION AND THE EDUCATION REVOLUTION

From 1996 to 2007, Australia was governed by a Liberal Coalition under the direction of Prime Minister John Howard. During that period, as the Federal Government continued to support and shape education policy, several key themes emerged.

There was an ongoing narrative that seemed to imply that Australian students were underperforming. In fact, the prime minister famously claimed that 30 percent of Australian students were not achieving adequate literacy standards (Cobbold, 2007). This was a dubious claim given that in the 2003 Programme for International Student Assessment (PISA), only 12 percent of Australian students were not achieving expected literacy standards compared to 19 percent for all OECD countries (OECD, 2003).

Despite these claims being easily debunked, the Howard government persisted with the narrative and implied that increasing levels of school choice and market driven accountability would improve the situation. While a popular claim of many governments who imply that increasing competition among schools will lead to better results, this is not a finding that has been conclusively validated by the educational research community. Howard's government also asserted that increased choice in education would lead to better outcomes for low-income families, as recurrent funding and capital grants for Independent schools would level the playing field for lower SES students, leading to increased school choice, student mobility, and improved student outcomes. Again, these results were more philosophical in nature and not led by any particular body of research.

In November 2007, Australians voted in a new Labor government led by Prime Minister Kevin Rudd, who subsequently appointed Julia Gillard as the education minister. Typically, once every decade, Australian Ministers of Education at both the federal and state level would gather to create goals and commit to actions in Education. This occurred in Hobart in 1989 and again in Adelaide in 1999. Hence, in 2008, a gathering of education ministers met to refresh their commitment to educational outcomes for the country.

Among the trends noted at the 2008 conference in Melbourne (Ministerial Council, 2008) were the impact on education of:

- *globalization, in terms of workforce mobility and global competitiveness;*
- *technological advancement and the need for technical literacy; and*
- *complex social and environmental issues such as climate change and increasing diversity.*

Also noted as an area of strength was Australia's fairly impressive standing with respect to its peer OECD nations in the PISA assessments, including a note about the 2006 results where young Australians cracked the top ten in all three educational domains measured (OECD, 2006). This was a stark contrast to the Howard government's inaccurate claims from a decade earlier. However, there was an easily understood tone in the document that historical PISA results were simply a starting point and there was an obsessive need for Australia to shatter previous high-water marks to challenge for dominance in education to combat the forces of globalization.

Alongside these stated goals on educational excellence was an undercurrent of dissatisfaction on the issue of equity. Director for Education at the OECD, Professor Barry McGaw, noticed that the most socially disadvantaged students in Australia lag about eighteen months to two years behind the reading ability of the poorest students in Canada, Japan, Finland, and South Korea. Despite holding pretensions to an egalitarian society, he stated that Australia's performance in educating its socially disadvantaged children was of a similar standard to the more entrenched class societies of Britain and the United States (McGaw, 2007). Thus, both excellence and equity would need to be addressed.

As a result of the conference, the Melbourne Declaration (Ministerial Council, 2008) articulated two goals for Australian Education:

1. *Australian schooling promotes equity and excellence.*
2. *All young Australians become successful learners, confident and creative individuals, and active and informed citizens.*

While these statements would not be seen as controversial, written into the declaration were subcomponents, which would dominate the educational conversation in the country for many years. These elements involved discussion of the goals with respect to improving equity, developing community partnerships, standardizing and enhancing curriculum, and assessing and enforcing system-wide accountability.

The Melbourne Declaration saw Australian schools not as standalone entities, but as integral partners with communities ready to serve as after school care providers or community gathering places. It articulated a connection between schools, businesses, and indigenous communities. This was a subtle reference at the time but the word "Partnerships" in Australian Education soon grew to include "National Partnerships": those government programs that school and school systems could participate in to achieve funding guarantees.

The Melbourne Declaration (Ministerial Council, 2008) stated:

> Learning areas are not of equal importance at all year levels. English and Mathematics are of fundamental importance in all years of schooling and are the primary focus of learning in the early years . . . . To ensure that student achievement is measured in meaningful ways, State, Territory and Commonwealth governments will work with all school sectors to develop and enhance national and school-level assessment.
>
> (p. 14)

These statements were crucial and foreshadowed much of what would follow. If the old axiom of what gets measured gets done would hold true, it was clear that English and mathematics curricula would dominate the next decade. The curricula would be driven by assessment of outcomes by state and territory authorities and a commonwealth government that had now formally inserted itself as an arbiter of world class curriculum and assessment.

In addition, rather than eschew former Prime Minister Howard's market-based approach to education, the Melbourne Declaration embraced and codified the message. Schools would be thrust into a competitive market-driven landscape where those who showed quick wins on standardized assessments would thrive.

The final subsection of the Melbourne Declaration dealt with strengthening accountability and transparency. What was now clear was that schools would need to deal with new actors in demonstrating performance. Historically, schools and parents communicated with, and trusted each other, to provide sound education to children. Now, information that was previously the private domain of teachers and parents was open to interpretation by the community and the government.

The Melbourne Declaration was not merely an aspirational document but rather an organization of the new Labor government's Education Revolution, a phrase which Rudd and Gillard began to popularize during their election campaign in 2007, with the promise of a $19.3B commitment to education in the 2008 fiscal budget (Gillard, 2008). The Labor government had hung their collective hats on education to transform the Australian economy from one based on natural resources to a highly developed tertiary economy ready to take on the challenges of globalization.

But what happens when a school attempts to govern itself toward policy ideals rather than more systemic concerns? When schools are reimagined as learning communities through which excellence and equity are seen to operate harmoniously amidst a marketization of educational services, the nature of schools changes. Schools are inherently systemic in nature; systems organize themselves over long periods of time to produce results that are efficient and reflect the norms, goals, and traditions of the community.

In the case of education in Australia, by 2006, the system was functioning quite well, though not perfectly. Results could have been more equitable and such inequities could have been addressed by defining inputs that could help in leveling the playing field and creating a less privileged approach. Similarly results could have been closer to excellent. If top-ten PISA results were not the desired threshold, international educational rankings could have been addressed by building the system's capacity to deliver a broad range of services.

Instead, market forces of competition, accountability, and transparency were introduced as mechanisms to promote the dual outcomes of equity and excellence. As Rudd and Gillard clearly articulated, equity and excellence are not incompatible, but as Savage (2011) suggested if the state chooses the architecture of advanced capitalism to produce the results, there would be winners and losers.

POLICY INITIATIVES

The task of operationalizing a National Education Strategy is daunting. With the stated goal of the Melbourne Declaration, to improve both equity and excellence in education, the Australian government required a mechanism to impact the stated outcomes. Consequently, in 2008, the Australian Curriculum, Assessment, and Reporting Authority (ACARA) was created (ACARA, 2018). Though the brainchild of the federal government, ACARA branded itself as an independent authority. One of the first mandates of ACARA was the creation of the Australian National Curriculum (ANC) as a way to impact equity across urban, rural, and remote regions of Australia.

Previously, each state or territory had its own curriculum and the imposition of a National Curriculum was considered a timely and heroic challenge. By 2014, a new national curriculum was unveiled across the country based on agreed-upon standards derived from an amalgam of previously existing practices across the states and new imperatives derived from a global competitiveness agenda (Ministerial Council, 2008). Full implementation from the foundations level (Pre-K) to Year 10 (grade 10 in North America) began by 2014, with subject-by-subject implementation moving ahead at the secondary level (ACARA, 2018). Certain exemptions and alternative curricula were produced, which considered outliers such as Montessori, Steiner, and International Baccalaureate programs.

The implementation of the National Curriculum was left under state and territory authority. Still, as a standardized document, it was uncertain if the ANC could be flexible enough to account for individual conditions that existed within states. The trend in modern curriculum development is emerging away from curricula, which consists of a mammoth basket of behavioral standards (Jacobsen & Saultz, 2012), hence some may argue that the ANC is actually a relic of educational standardization, as countries such as Germany and Finland move to more flexible, inquiry-based approaches (Kotthoff & Terhart, 2013).

Though impressively managed as a project, the ANC also highlighted the changing nature of federalism in Australia, raising questions such as; if curriculum is national, would education in any form still be a provincial concern? The argument extends beyond Australia's borders as many nations grapple with global competitiveness agendas and address these issues through national strategies.

For example, can a national strategy best serve the needs of a country, given that local concerns may take precedence? Is a six-year-old child raised in a mining community in rural Australia expected to master a set of standards more tailored for an inner-city child in Sydney, who has access to a different set of experiences and resources? The answer to those questions may have emerged in the implementation of the ANC by each state. Through a process of acknowledging different circumstances and massaging various expectations, each state might have been able to use a national curriculum document to best meet the needs of their children. However, this freedom of implementation was usurped by the development of a parallel national testing system.

To monitor the implementation of the ANC and to ensure progress toward their goals of excellence, ACARA developed the National Assessment Program, Literacy and Numeracy (NAPLAN). Through NAPLAN, students would be tested in Years 3, 5, 7, and 9 on literacy and numeracy (National Assessment Program [NAP], 2016). The tests are standardized in nature and come with all of the traditional benefits and flaws in standardized tests. The benefits of standardized testing are that they do an excellent job of ranking students (Tanner, 2013). Based on a basket of topics, a savvy test maker can produce an instrument that is both valid and reliable in dividing a class into quartiles based on achievement. The downfall of a standardized test is that it can provide no information as to why the spread in quartiles exist.

And as the ANC was based on behavioral standards, a standardized assessment could only define the behavior on a particular day and in a specific set of circumstances. Still, in the right hands, the analysis of items from a standardized test can produce useful information to informed educators talented at using standardized assessments as a small part of a student's overall assessment. Publishing high stakes test results to the general publish proved problematic as it left group data open to interpretation by users unsophisticated with its analysis. Yet ACARA's political origins made the push toward open results inevitable.

With an agenda of accountability and transparency in mind, ACARA created the MySchool website, an online portal whereby stakeholders could compare and contrast school-level-standardized test results to neighboring schools. MySchool would make all NAPLAN scores publicly available. Local media outlets would hasten every year to transcribe NAPLAN data from the website into their local papers to produce league tables of winning and losing schools. ACARA failed to understand that branding schools as losers branded the teachers, students, and parents as losers as well.

With little or no context available and no ability for schools to qualify results for small sample sizes or other additional environmental factors, school practices would change from a robust implementation of the ANC to an approach that focused on raising NAPLAN results in relation to peer schools. As is the case with most jurisdictions that attempt standardized testing, a narrowing of the curriculum occurred, which minimized student-centered approaches (David, 2011). MySchool only exacerbated this effect by accelerating each school's response to the data in order to allay parental concerns or highlight easy to measure outcomes, over more complex learning behaviors.

AITSL: EDUCATOR STANDARDS

The Australian Institute for Teaching and School Leadership (AITSL) was founded in 2010 with an aim for articulating standards for both teachers and principals (AITSL, 2017). At first glance, this may have seemed to be one additional set of expectations in a country reeling from the effects of educational reform. However, in stark contrast to the types of reform efforts imposed on schools and children, AITSL's charge was to build system-wide capacity rather than punish existing school leaders. This was done through an analysis of individual school performance. The goal of AITSL was not simply standardization, but the development of a professional, evidence-informed teaching and school leadership workforce that understood and improved its own impact on learning (AITSL, 2017a).

The current chair of AITSL, John Hattie, author of *Visible Learning for Teachers: Maximizing Impact on Learning* (2008), which used a meta-analysis to determine effect sizes of various environmental and programmatic factors in schools, brought a research focus to AITSL that values study, scholarship, and measured implementation. AITSL has focused its charge on initial teacher certification and the provision of ongoing professional learning. In concert with state colleges of teachers, AITSL supports its standards with tools designed to improve educator effectiveness. The result has been an increased perception of and emphasis on teacher professionalism.

In addition to influencing teacher preparation, a large part of AITSL's work has been focused on the identification, recruitment, preparation, and development of school principals. School leadership has been a looming crisis in Australia for the past decade. As early as 2007, various agencies have identified leadership as an area of opportunity that could be used to influence Australia's system of education (Anderson et al., 2007). A demographic change was taking place that saw the retirement of a large proportion of existing school principals. Younger principals were reporting they felt underprepared for their roles, and in particular, that of instructional leadership, critical in the implementation of new national curriculum and teacher-effectiveness standards.

A recent AITSL publication, *Leading for Impact: Australian Guidelines for School Leadership Development* (AITSL, 2017b), is seen as a positive contribution in the awareness of the impact school leaders have on education because it examined not only school management and continuity but also the causal effect of improving student outcomes by choosing and monitoring the effects of pedagogical methods (AITSL, 2017).

A further emphasis of AITSL has been to intentionally increase the proportion of women in school leadership positions. In relation to the proportion of female teachers, there has been an under-representation at the school leadership level (Little, 2017). If outstanding female educators have felt disenfranchised from pursuing school leadership roles, it diminishes the overall capacity of the school system to deliver quality instruction.

The link between school performance and school leadership continues to be demonstrated (Barber, Whelan, & Clark, 2010). Unlike other reforms present during the education revolution, one could argue the formation of AITSL and its emphasis on building the capacity and effectiveness of human resources may be the most transformational in the long run. Often seen as an aside to the reforms arising from the Melbourne Declaration focused on PISA results, standardized tests, and national curricula, the impact of AITSL as a national body devoted to improving school communities will have the most long-lasting impact.

Still, while AITSL is structured to create a lasting impact in Australian Education, it curiously seems to have organized itself at arm's length from the educators it serves. Unlike ACARA that has grown from its Independent roots to embrace input from all states and territories, AITSL has centralized its power to a handful of federally appointed experts. This inability of AITSL to democratically represent and learn from the Australian educational community may be its downfall. Australians have little tolerance for institutions that are perceived as noninclusive, arbitrary, or unfair.

Building the Education Revolution

The timing of the Australian government's 2007 pronouncement of the Education Revolution and the ensuing 2008 Melbourne Declaration were both unfortunate and convenient given the coinciding global economic crises. By 2009, it became clear that some investment in government spending would be required to stimulate economies around the world. In Australia, this led the federal government to justify a large-scale capital building program targeting school facilities for additions and improvement. Given the Rudd government's commitment to education, schools seemed like a logical target for government investment. The program was named Building the Education Revolution (BER).

Over a three-year period, the Australian government invested over $16B in improving both government and nongovernment school facilities. An injection of such a magnitude in an education system that operates in terms of decades-long planning horizons was problematic. No school administrator wanted to waste the opportunity to add capital improvements to their schools, but the shortened time frame of the rollout created various inequities, as in each sector, government, Independent, and Catholic schools needed to follow different routes to access BER funds.

To sell the investment to the public, government officials would use the idea of "Community Partnerships" spelled out in the Melbourne Declaration to connect the school projects back to the community (ACER, 2010). Rather than favoring the replacement of an outdated classroom, projects that integrated school activities with their community were prioritized. A school hall, library, or related asset that could serve the community was favored over a project that simply added value for the students. Therefore, many times the projects chosen were strategic in nature with an aim to advance those that had a greater likelihood to be approved for funding, rather than what the community or the students actually required.

Pundits have debated the relative merits of the BER campaign. As early as 2010, after the Education Minister Julia Gillard ousted Kevin Rudd in the Prime Minister's chair, opposition governments called for task forces to investigate the misappropriation of government funds through the BER. Successive inquiries into the program have failed to turn up any systemic level of corruption or inefficiency. As a capital works project, the BER was considered a marginal success both by economists and school leaders when compared to previous federal infrastructure projects (Lewis, Dollery, & Kortt, 2014).

An important consideration not to be overlooked is that this comprehensive level of public investment was overseen primarily by school principals. School leaders, many of whom were reeling from a great deal of change in the education system, were tasked with the implementation of a program designed to combat the global economic crisis and reinvigorate a stalled Australian economy. The execution and project management of the BER were left to school officials; an enormous and underrated contribution by the education system.

Coinciding with the BER program, several studies began to emerge that showed increasing levels of stress among school principals in Australia. School principals are responsible for managing schools, coordinating and guiding teaching, networking with external partners, and communicating with parents.

In addition, they are accountable for administration and finances, personnel management, and are legally responsible for all issues that arise in their schools. Finally, they have a pedagogical role to play, ensuring student learning, competency development, and student assessment. They must collaborate with education bureaucracies, undergo regular inspections, play a leading role in implementing curricular innovations, and connect with other supporting services beyond the school itself.

The negative effects of this immense increase in responsibility were demonstrated in a 2016 national survey (Riley, Beausart, Froehlich, & Devos, 2016), which showed a worrying trend among Australian school principals with respect to their mental health. The study showed that the level of stress among Australian principals continued to increase in Independent, Catholic, and state-run schools. Sleeping problems for Australian school leaders were shown to be 2.2 times the general population.

Furthermore, depression, burnout, and traumatic stress had nearly doubled from historic levels; in fact, all of the indicators that somebody is not coping very well were prevalent in principals. This may coincide with public trust in the education system being eroded (Riley et al., 2016). According to Riley, "When you have one in five principals showing serious signs of distress then we have a systemic problem, not an individual problem" (Robinson, 2018).

The BER can be explored at a macroeconomic level on the basis of its efficiency as a government spending program. In this regard, there are contrasting interpretations; overall, it is considered no less efficient than previous instances of government spending. However, the analysis of the BER has seldom been analyzed from a systems perspective.

Important questions to consider are: Did the overall program improve student outcomes in Australia? Did it contribute to stress and uncertainty among school leaders? Did it interfere with the natural planning horizon that school systems generally use when deciding on capital projects? As in most instances in education, the overall effect will not be measured for many years. Too often, the effect of such programs on the overall education system is minimized.

REVISITING THE FUNDING MODEL FOR ALL SCHOOLS IN AUSTRALIA

In 2010, then Education Minister and soon to be Prime Minister Julia Gillard commissioned a report from heralded Australian business leader David Gonski on the funding of Australian schools (Gonski et al, 2011). The goal of the report was to ensure that all schools in Australia were fairly funded to an adequate level, which would ensure that the lofty goals emerging from the Melbourne Declaration would be met. As previously outlined in this chapter, the focus of the Education Revolution in Australia was on the dual goals of both excellence and equity with the key term of "accountability" permeating the process to achieve both outcomes.

Gonski's report was delivered to Prime Minister Gillard in early 2012. Eight months later, its 41 recommendations became public. In simplest terms, the report called for $5B per year to be injected into the education sector (Gonski, 2011). To meet this recommendation, Gillard committed $14.5B over six years from the federal government with the remaining to be made up by a 3 percent increase in state- or territory-government allocations. The task was then to sell each state on the agreement. The states were reluctant to commit. It may have been that they saw an election on the horizon and were wary about agreeing to a commitment that may not be honored by the next federal government. Eventually, four states and the Australian Capital Territory agreed to the Gonski's funding formula, and it was implemented nationally through a series of complex deals involving various states, territories, and private agencies.

The Gonski report was a document rooted in Australian ideology; it did not shy away from public or private contributions and attempted to set a fair path toward school funding. If there was a threshold amount that typically led to desired outcomes, then legislating a minimum standard close to that amount seemed appropriate. Gonski's funding model was generally praised for its commitment to low SES schools and students, and for additional funds provided for students with disabilities.

Its critics pointed to a perceived lack of transparency in its complicated system of loadings that referred to data that may have been volatile, opaque, and in some cases, simply not available. Perhaps the most troubling component was not the Gonski recommendations but the process by which the states would play politics in determining its implementation. In order to advance the Gonski recommendations, state and territory governments would need to agree to the funding model and with each successive agreement it was left to the imagination what was negotiated between the Commonwealth and the state. This lack of transparency created a public mistrust for special deals and resulted in a lack of buy-in for the reform.

OUTCOMES

Despite eight years of school-funding debates in Australia aimed at creating a fairer and more equitable school resource standard, the issues of excellence and equity have not changed. In 2015, PISA results (OECD, 2015) showed that Australia had not only remained behind target nations such as Japan, Korea, Canada, and Finland in all domains, but it had regressed significantly since 2006, converging much closer to the OECD average.

This perceived lack of progress may be attributable to a lack of time provided for the common funding agreements to take hold. But perhaps it underscores what kinds of systems produce innovative results. The focus in Australian Education for the past decade has been on school funding and accountability. In both cases, there has been a trend to centralization in each of these dimensions.

As a result, Australia's education system has become far more inflexible. Standards have been centralized, curriculum has been standardized, funding has been defined, and outcomes have been measured. The timing of this trend to centralization and standardization seems to contradict that many educational jurisdictions have purposely injected experimentation and innovation into their own systems. Standardization in education is seen by many as an outdated relic of a factory model of education, which stood ready to produce benchmark results. Today's call for twenty-first-century skills requires innovative new models that necessitate insulation from constant system-wide assessment to produce new ways of thinking.

Many educators predict that brick and mortar schools will no longer exist in their current format in twenty years, having been augmented with online learning, artificial intelligence, and individualized student programming. The Gonski funding process, in its quest for fairness, turned the conversation to equity and away from excellence. Ultimately, through the Education Revolution, Australia has now defined a fairer and more replicable process to govern its school systems; however, whether it is better for Australian children remains to be seen.

A CURRENT AUSTRALIAN PERSPECTIVE: 2018

From the perspective of those endeavoring to operate within Australian education, the period of the Education Revolution was tumultuous, with reform agendas piled upon teachers and principals at an unprecedented rate. The reform movement was rolled out amid the uncertainty of dramatically dynamic politics as successive governments and prime ministerships have come and gone in Australia over the past decade, more often through bitter internal divisions than at the behest of the electorate.

Perhaps because of weariness and skepticism that any government initiative will last long enough to make a difference, the impetus for reform has dwindled from the lofty original goals of equity and excellence to an obsessive focus on funding alone. The funding debate has been exacerbated by media and union-driven efforts to name and shame "over-funded" schools.

In addition, growing divisions between the Catholic and Independent sectors have fueled the issue. Finally, the political spectacle of the Labor Party championing, compromising, and then opposing their own Gonski reforms in response to the Liberal Party opposing, abandoning, and then adopting them has left the public confused about the debate's original intention.

At the same time, the role and profile of AITSL has diminished, as has the stature of ACARA, all of them significantly defunded since 2013. Ongoing development of the ANC has also lost momentum following what was widely perceived to have been an ideologically motivated review launched by the short-lived Abbott Government. The review never appeared to deliver a discernible outcome but served to tarnish the credibility of the whole ANC endeavor and thereby licensed the states and territories to retain their own emphases rather than continue striving toward national unity.

Similarly, the unpopularity of NAPLAN has been compounded by a logistically ill-prepared attempt to transfer the assessments to an online platform that had to be abandoned only weeks before the start of nationwide tests in 2017. The debacle squandered the efforts of teachers and resources of schools around the country and fueled calls for the scheme to be dropped entirely. That chorus has recently culminated in the very public repudiation of

NAPLAN by the education ministers of several states and territories. Meanwhile, Australia's PISA results have continued to fall (OECD, 2015)

Despite the upset associated with reform implementation, there are glimmers of a renewed commitment to educational reform emerging from the tangle of the Education Revolution. Having surprised the nation in May 2017 by suddenly committing to the previously abandoned Gonski report, the Turnbull government also commissioned David Gonski to lead a second review into the means of achieving educational excellence, which was characterized as a guide to effective educational spending and to reversing Australia's perceived PISA crisis.

Delivered in March 2018, only seven months after its commissioning, the report could hardly match the groundbreaking quality of its predecessor, and much of its content has been criticized for relative vagueness. Nonetheless, it has shifted the discourse at last from funding to teaching, learning, and leadership, with a clear focus on creating conditions for capacity building in schools, not just measuring performance in hopes that accountability alone will drive improvement.

It is too early to anticipate the likely effects of the proposals or their chances of being realized under Australia's politically divided federalist system. Nonetheless, they signal movement beyond funding arguments toward the opportunity for a new national discourse on education, which may leave behind the turmoil of the Education Revolution to enter a new phase of more careful, sustainable, and enduring evolution.

CONCLUSION

Systems analysis tells us that policy-based reforms will struggle to gain traction within complex national systems such as education. The Australian Education Revolution was no exception.

Characteristics of the period included

- a dual agenda to simultaneously influence both equity and excellence in the current education system;
- the continuing evolution of education from a state concern to one that promoted a unified national political agenda;
- a narrative that championed education to mitigate the effects of globalization and improve economic competitiveness;
- an increasingly standardized and centralized treatment of curricular objectives in a nation consisting of disparate regional concerns;
- a flawed system of national testing inconsistent with Australian norms and unpopular across the country;

- a well-intentioned national school building campaign, which saw education as a legitimate player in addressing economic policy;
- an important debate on school funding that took a decade to implement and ultimately ended in compromise rather than transformation; and
- an innovative capacity-building approach to improving teacher and principal effectiveness, producing promising early returns, but with a troubling unrepresentative governance structure that may mitigate its impact.

The five-year period of educational reform from 2008 to 2013 will have a lasting impact on Australian education and Australian federalism. Although many of the reforms did not lead to their intended outcomes, such as improved national standardized test results or higher ranking on PISA in relation to peer OECD countries, the analysis is much more complex.

The Education Revolution placed a renewed emphasis on curriculum across the country, rebuilt physical infrastructure, enhanced the professionalism of educators, and led to a re-examination of the relationship between the Commonwealth and state governments. Though harried and painful at times, the lessons learned and capacity built may prove to be invaluable as Australia continues its growth as a leading economic and political nation. If the Australian Education Revolution is viewed as the first colony in a grand educational experiment, we should not be surprised by the amazing fruit it may eventually bear.

REFERENCES

ACER: Australian Council for Educational Research (2010, November). *School—Community partnerships in Australian Schools*. Retrieved from https://research.acer.edu.au/cgi/viewcontent.cgi?article=1006&context=policy_analysis_misc

AITSL: Australian Institute for Teaching and School Leadership. (2017a). Retrieved from https://www.aitsl.edu.au/

AITSL: Australian Institute for Teaching and School Leadership. (2017b, December). *Leading for Impact: Australian guidelines for school leadership development. Victoria, Australia*. Retrieved from http://apo.org.au/node/135786

Anderson, M., Gronn, P., Ingvarson, L., Jackson, A., Kleinhenz, E., McKenzie, P., Thornton, N. (2007). *OECD improving school leadership activity: Australia country background Report*. Australia Council for Educational Research. Canberra City, Australia. Retrieved from http://www.oecd.org/education/school/39967643.pdf

Australian Curriculum, Assessment, and Reporting Authority. (2018). *Overview*. Retrieved from https://www.acara.edu.au/about-us

Barber, M., Whelan, F., & Clark, M. (2010). Capturing the leadership premium. *McKinsey & Company*. Retrieved from https://www.mckinsey.com/industries/social-sector/our-insights/capturing-the-leadership-premium

Cobbold, T. (2007). *The great school fraud: Howard government school education policy 1996–2006. A paper prepared for the Australian Education Union.* Retrieved from http://www.saveourschools.com.au/national-issues/the-great-school-fraud

Cumming, J. J., & Mawdsley, R. (2012). The nationalisation of education in Australia and annexation of private schooling to public goals. *International Journal of Law and Education, 17*(2), 7–31.

David, J. (2011). Research says. . . . High stakes testing narrows curriculum. *Educational Leadership, 68*(6), 78–80.

Devine, L. D. (1991). State aid for education in Australia: An overview. In D. S. Penner (Ed.), *Public funds and private education: Issues of church and state.* Paper presented at the North American Division of Seventh-day Adventists Education—PARL Conference, Clackamas, 17–18 June (pp. 31–40). Silver Spring, MD: North American Division of Seventh-day Adventists Office of Education. Retrieved from https://research.avondale.edu.au/cgi/viewcontent.cgi?article=1000&context=admin_papers

Gillard, J. (2008, August 27). Education revolution in our schools. *Ministers Media Center.* Retrieved from https://ministers.jobs.gov.au/gillard/education-revolution-our-schools

Gonski, D., Boston, K., Greiner, K., Lawrence, C., Scales, B., & Tannock, P. (2011). Review of funding for schooling: Final report. *Department of Education, Employment and Workplace Relations. Canberra City, Australia.* Retrieved from https://docs.education.gov.au/system/files/doc/other/review-of-funding-for-schooling-final-report-dec-2011.pdf

Harrington, M. (2011). Australian government funding explained. *Parliamentary Library.* Retrieved from https://www.aph.gov.au/binaries/library/pubs/bn/sp/schoolsfunding.pdf

Jacobsen, R., & Saultz, A. (2012). The polls—Trends: Who should control education? *Public Opinion Quarterly, 76*(2), 379–390.

Karmel, P. (1973, May). *Schools in Australia. Report of the Interim Committee for the Australian School Commission.* Retrieved from http://apo.org.au/node/29669

Kotthoff, H. G., & Terhart, E. (2013). New solutions to old problems? Recent reforms in teacher education in Germany. *Revista Espanola de Educacion Comparada, 22*, 73–92.

Lamb, S., Jackson, J., Walstab, A., & Huo, S. (2015). *Educational opportunity in Australia 2015: Who succeeds and who missed out?* Melbourne, Australia: Center for International Research on Education Systems for the Mitchell Institute.

Lewis, C., Dollery, B., & Kortt, M. (2014). Building the education revolution: Another case of Australian government failure? *International Journal of Public Administration, 37*(5), 299–307.

Little, G. (2017, November 20). Program to lure more women in school leadership. *Education HQ.* Retrieved from https://au.educationhq.com/news/44451/program-to-lure-more-women-into-school-leadership

McGaw, B. (2007, December 8). The race is not always the richest. *The Economist.*

Ministerial Council on Education, Employment, Training and Youth Affairs (Australia). (2008). *Melbourne declaration on educational goals for young Australians.* Retrieved from http://nla.gov.au/nla.arc-93985

MinistersMediaCenter.(2008, August27).*Educationrevolutioninourschools*.Retrieved from https://ministers.jobs.gov.au/gillard/education-revolution-our-schools

National Assessment Program. (2016). *About.* Retrieved from https://www.nap.edu.au/about

Nationmaster. (2018). *Facts and stats about Australia.* Retrieved from https://www.nationmaster.com/country-info/profiles/Australia

Organisation for Economic Co-operation and Development. (2003). *First results from PISA 2003: Executive summary.* Paris, France: Author. Retrieved from http://www.oecd.org/education/school/programmeforinternationalstudentassessment-pisa/34002454.pdf

Organisation for Economic Co-operation and Development. (2006). *PISA 2006: Science competencies for tomorrow's world.* Paris, France: Author. Retrieved from http://www.oecd.org/education/school/programmeforinternationalstudentassessmentpisa/pisa2006results.htm

Organisation for Economic Co-operation and Development. (2015). *PISA 2015.* Paris, France: Author. Retrieved from https://www.oecd.org/pisa/pisa-2015-results-in-focus.pdf

Riley, P., Beausart, S., Froehlich, D., & Devos, C. (2016). Effects of support on stress and Burnout on Australian principals. *Educational Research, 58*(4), 347–365.

Robinson, N. (2018, February 20). *School principals at higher risk of burnout, depression due to workplace stress, survey finds.* Retrieved from https://www.abc.net.au/news/2018-02-21/principals-overwhelmed-by-workplace-stress-acu-survey-finds/9468078

Rowe, E. (2017). *Australian country case study.* Paper commissioned for the 2017/8 Global Education Monitoring Report, Accountability in education: Meeting our Commitments. United Nations Educational, Scientific and Cultural Organization. Retrieved from http://unesdoc.unesco.org/images/0025/002595/259541e.pdf

Tanner, J. (2013). *The pitfalls of reform: Its incompatibility with actual improvement.* Lanham, Maryland. R&L Education

Tourism Australia. (2018). *Facts and planning: Australia's history.* Retrieved from https://www.australia.com/en/facts-and-planning/history.html

Chapter Three

School Leadership in Ethiopia

Reinventing the Principalship through Locally Responsive Practices

Abebayehu Tekleselassie

Amaarah DeCuir

Across sub-Saharan Africa, schooling and education are changing rapidly as countries strive to respond to the new demands of the Millennium Development Goals (United Nations [UN], 2000). Developed by the UN in 2000, this project established societal goals for member nations, including providing universal primary education for all children. Under a context of inequitable schooling access, poor literacy rates, and gender inequality, this initiative ushered in new priorities for national governments and local school leaders.

Although many countries are under-resourced, poorly funded, and struggle to generate policy changes that address social justice issues of equity and access, they prioritized the establishment of universal primary education because it had the greatest likelihood of increasing quality of life across the region. Decades later, in response to these international goals, many African nations have increased access to primary education, reduced illiteracy rates, and advanced gender parity through policy changes and societal advancements.

Across the continent, African governments embraced the work necessary to achieve the Millennium Development Goals, recognizing that education positions nations, and its people, to be competitive on the global stage (Bush, 2009). Education also impacts communities and individuals by facilitating personal and social transformations (Bush, 2009). Although national policies must reflect changing priorities, the local schools and their leaders would bear the increased demands on school access and equity (Bush, 2009). African governments and ministries of education often referenced existing scholarly literature to construct national plans for school leadership development and preparation.

Education leadership scholarship is rooted in Western perspectives, Western theories, and Western sites of data collection and analysis. Although much of what is known of education leadership is regarded as universal best practices, scholars have asserted that effective leadership is tethered to a local context (Van de Westhuizen & Vuuren, 2007). African concepts and practices of school leadership serve African communities; the scholarship derived from these contexts is best suited for situating a local understanding and base of knowledge.

Research grounded in an African context will help examine how African school leaders make sense of their work by foregrounding African concepts, practices, and cultural understandings. Li (2012) defined indigenous management research as "any study on a unique local phenomenon, or a unique element of any local phenomenon from a local (native as emic) perspective to explore its local implications, and if possible, its global implications as well" (p. 851). This is not achieved by comparing and contrasting African schooling contexts with those situated in the West, but rather using African concepts to describe African contexts without international comparisons.

Drawing on an African education leadership study, Sperandio and Merab Kagoda (2010) asserted that there is a need to formulate indigenous and non-Western theories of educational leadership that are grounded in research that accounts for and explains indigenous ways of knowing and leading. Adding to the contested assertions, Tsui (2004) claimed that indigenous research requires location-specific contextual factors that must be native to the local population, although the theoretical lens can be borrowed from elsewhere. Whetton (2009) suggested that any research can be labeled as indigenous if it covers an indigenous phenomenon or topic, even if theories or concepts are adopted.

Recognizing that Africa itself is a diverse land with many nations of people, Ethiopia serves as a case to understand the implications of school leadership and leadership development, as well as missed opportunities for success. Ethiopia sought to prepare for the Millennium Development Goals (UN, 2000) through a decentralization process to empower local leadership, complemented by the implementation of a national set of leadership preparation standards to better position school leaders as agents of change as they advanced new national priorities.

This chapter explores leadership development in Ethiopia through the shift in educational governance and the advancement of universal primary education. It is our hope that by centering African concepts and knowledge through scholarly research, our work will more effectively make meaning of indigenous leadership, preparation, and policy implementation in Ethiopia.

RECRUITMENT OF AFRICAN SCHOOL LEADERS

Across many parts of Africa, school leaders are appointed from among the teaching faculty of a school. They are commonly referred to as "headteachers," a term rooted in English colonial legacy. Headteachers are recognized as the administrative and managerial leaders of a school; they are usually appointed from among the school's more experienced teachers, with an implicit understanding that this experience satisfies the preparation needed to be a headteacher (Bush & Glover, 2016).

In some cases, people are appointed as headteachers for political connections, nepotism, or ethnic or cultural identities, often without prior classroom teaching experiences (Bush & Glover, 2016). The appointment process is managed by noneducators, often regional government administrators, without sufficient understanding of school leadership (Bush & Glover, 2016; Bush & Oduro, 2006). The path to becoming a headteacher in Africa is inconsistent. Some are appointed without having applied, others years after their initial application; some have less than 10 years of teaching, others have more than 20 years in the classroom (Onguko, Abdalla, & Webber, 2012). These inconsistencies contribute to the perception that the route to school leadership in African nations is neither professionalized nor standardized.

Once assigned to a position of school leadership, headteachers generally prefer to function as the administrative and managerial leaders of their schools, de-emphasizing the role of instructional leader (Oplatka, 2004). Instead, in assuming only the administrative and managerial roles of school leadership, they emphasize tasks that can be completed over visionary concepts that must be established (Bush & Oduro, 2006). This is a result of specific education policies within Ethiopia enacted at the national level and implemented locally. First, headteachers are often appointed for a single year term and then must be re-elected by the faculty to extend their term of service.

As such, many leaders do not intend to remain in their position very long, so they hesitate to invest time and energy to large sweeping initiatives. Second, the path toward school leadership often begins in the classroom and does not include preparation for organizational learning, strategic planning, or transformational leadership. Rather, leaders are placed directly from the classroom into a brief, informational training before assuming authority as a school leader.

There is little understanding about the impacts of recruitment strategies without associated leadership preparation on the performance of school leaders. Research from West Africa indicated that the absence of preparation programs caused leaders to rely on models of school leadership from their own personal experiences (Bush & Glover, 2016).

Either following the example of the leader installed in the school when they were a teacher or reaching back further to emulate the school leader responsible for them as a student, leaders without formal preparation are left trying to mimic leadership practices rather than visioning new possibilities. One educator said, "If teachers experience only traditional, top down, managerial leadership approaches, it is unsurprising that, in the absence of specific training, they reproduce this style when they are appointed as principals" (Bush & Glover, 2016).

Although such an informal apprenticeship experience might yield moderate success in a stable environment, school leaders are facing unchartered territory as globalization, climate, geographical, and social changes are contributing to significant changes across communities and schools. As such, school leaders positioned in African contexts confront changing school landscapes without strategies or tools to meet the critical needs of students, staff, or communities.

AFRICAN SCHOOL LEADERSHIP

Once appointed, school leaders confront compelling socio-geo-economic factors, often situated outside of the school and unique to the African context, that impact their leadership (Bush & Glover, 2016). Addressing these conditions requires specific preparation beyond teaching experience to effectively lead a school.

In this region of the world, there are devastating challenges that directly impact a leader's ability to manage a school. There are abject poverty and killer diseases, which threaten the health and well-being of students, teachers, and community members in developing countries (Bush, 2009). This includes HIV/AIDS, which impacts the health and viability of family members, children of famine who require additional nutritional resources to address their basic living needs, and children stricken with severe diseases who need consistent access to medical care (Onguko et al., 2012). School leaders have access to limited human and material resources to feed and care for their students, leaving them with a population that is significantly weakened, yet one they are still accountable to educate (Bush, 2009).

The geographical landscape of East Africa is predominantly wide with expansive rural lands that are sparsely populated. The population depends on an agricultural economic system that is significantly influenced by rainfall, drought, and harvests. This contributes to a poor, mostly illiterate, community base surrounding schools. The local population struggles to support the education process or the schools because they do not recognize the need for this pursuit of knowledge in the lives of their children.

At the same time, the urban centers are populated by upper- and middle-income families with more consistent access to social and economic resources, as well as educational opportunities. Despite these diverse concerns, educational leaders in East Africa are facing increasing accountability pressures to improve student achievement from parents, community members, and governmental administrators (Bush, 2009).

These challenges require leaders to demonstrate a full understanding of social justice, democracy, and equity in the operation of schools situated in developing countries (Spring, 2001; Young, Mountford, & Skria, 2006). Without sufficient resources and professional support, many leaders feel incapable of meeting these expectations; they demand additional training and adequate resources to strengthen their leadership capacity to promote equitable educational opportunities for their communities.

Globalization is an international force that impacts education resources in East Africa. This region provides a refuge for displaced people of neighboring countries due to war, famine, drought, as well as new economic opportunities. Leaders in this region must manage social, medical, political, and economic concerns that impact the lives of students and staff members (Scott & Rarieya, 2011). This has quickly produced a multiethnic, multilingual society within African schools (Scott & Rarieya, 2011).

East African countries are mitigating social issues such as determination of national language and language of instruction, management of immigrant and refugee movement, as well as an increase in crime and poverty as a result of globalization (Bush & Glover, 2009, 2016). Global influences have contributed to a diminishing role for parents and family, an increase in individualization among youth, and diverse beliefs on the role of religion in daily life. Despite these challenges, it is essential that leaders remain fully engaged with their communities and help decrease these socio-economic burdens (Bush, Kiggundu, & Moorosi, 2011).

Globalization has also brought an increased awareness from international donors seeking opportunities to leverage support for East African schools. This support often comes in the form of international aid and development programs directly associated with expectations to increase performance through national performance-based measure. In addition to funding, international donors are influencing East African education by supplanting indigenous education with curriculum and instructional techniques produced in developed countries. School leaders are required to manage these changing expectations with limited resources, ineffective local institutions, and a general unfamiliarity with international instructional resources.

Within the schools, leaders are facing unique difficulties that challenge their leadership. Schools have poor infrastructures and weak utility resources, contributing to physical and operational obstacles that are hard to manage

(Bush, 2009). Schools are becoming unsafe institutions due to increasing criminal activities, requiring schools to implement safety and security measures to protect students and staff in local area (Bush & Glover, 2009, 2016).

It is not possible to seek support from local governments because of a devolution of powers across national, regional, and local bureaucracies that weaken the school leader's ability to bring meaningful change (Bush, 2009). Although the changing policy landscape has given school leaders more autonomy and the organizational culture of a school is regarded as under the influence of the leader, their ability to implement strategic management in their schools remains limited by lack of funding and available resources as well as a general lack of leadership capacity (Bush & Glover, 2009; Moloi & Bush, 2006).

The workload for East African school leaders continues to increase, without additional resources to manage the growing demands on their time and resources (Bush & Oduro, 2006). They struggle to create an effective work-life balance because they do not have administrative or managerial support resources within a large, bureaucratic school system (Webber, Mentz, Scott, Mola Okoko, & Scott, 2014). School leaders are the ones responsible for ensuring the best allocation of available resources, both physical and human (Bush & Glover, 2009).

Leaders complain that they are not able to delegate work to other staff because there are no assistant administrators, just the leader (Bush & Oduro, 2006). One region did confirm the use of a school management committee to manage the school that involved a small team led by the school leader (Onguko et al., 2008). Some leaders described that they are required to maintain their teaching responsibilities while assuming administrative leadership of the school (Bush & Glover, 2016).

Leaders shared that they feel isolated in their work, from both staff and the community, because of the increasing workload and inability to delegate (Webber et al., 2014). These conditions contribute to the increased professional responsibilities of East African school leaders.

School leaders in East Africa are expected to lead through new, compelling experiences that they did not encounter in their former role as classroom teachers. School leaders face expanded responsibilities today beyond what was previously required of the position. No longer can a school leader simply manage the budget and supervise teachers; there is an increased demand on their workload to meet the new expectations of the position.

There are increasingly complex contextual changes that impact the lives of students, their families, and their communities. Leaders need to mitigate socio-geo-political terrain to operate their schools successfully and create conditions for students to learn. These demands require the professionalization of school leadership to create conditions by which school leaders are recognized for the unique requirements of their rapidly changing role in schools.

AFRICAN LEADERSHIP DEVELOPMENT

In order to meet these new expectations, school leaders must utilize leadership, administrative, and policy skills beyond what they have gained as experienced classroom teachers. Although there is widespread agreement in the region that leaders make a significant difference in schools, there is much less agreement as to how to develop effective leadership behaviors (Bush et al., 2011). The evidence confirms that school leadership demands an expertise unique to the position and situated in the changing contextual environment (Tekleselassie, 2002). In East Africa, there is an implicit risk that international donor support for education initiatives will also be associated with influencing preparation and development of school leaders. This is likely to structure educational leadership programs according to models and practices associated with school leadership in Western or developed countries. Contexts matter and the localization of knowledge is essential.

Because of this, it is critical that all efforts to strengthen school leadership in East Africa be rooted in indigenous research and models that reflect the socio-geo-political context of the region (Eacott & Asuga, 2014). The following sections describe how school leaders in East Africa are currently learning how to meet their expectations and then explore leadership development and preparation programs designed to enhance the performance of school leaders.

Across Africa, there persists an understanding that a school leader is equivalent to a headteacher, and that the sole prerequisite is experience as a classroom teacher (Bush & Glover, 2016). There is limited recognition that this is a specialized role that requires expertise beyond classroom teaching (Bush & Glover, 2016). Because of this, there is a significant absence of induction opportunities for school leaders (Bush & Oduro, 2006). Most simply gain their skills by mimicking the school leader who supervised them when they were a classroom teacher (Bush & Glover, 2016). This serves as an informal apprenticeship program that is limited by the leader's prior experiences as an observing classroom teacher. Others learn experientially on the job with an immediate placement and real-time expectations to lead (Bush & Oduro, 2006).

In some parts of East Africa, school leaders are first appointed as assistants before being assigned to lead their own schools (Onguko et al., 2008). This appears to be an ideal option that is not consistently implemented across the region. With a growing recognition that school leadership demands a new set of professional skills, it becomes necessary that leadership preparation and development programs flourish in East Africa.

It is not practical to remove all current school leaders and replace them with well-trained leaders to improve the quality of education in East Africa. Instead, research has confirmed that relevancy of leadership development programs is determined by their ability to increase capacity for those who are currently working as school leaders.

This is best accomplished with principles of active learning, usually in a workshop or seminar format, that enable leaders to immediately transfer new skills to their school context (Bush et al., 2011). Peer mentoring can be another form of effective leadership development. By carefully matching professionals and allocating sufficient time for mentoring, peers can support one another's leadership by sharing experiences and discussing leadership decisions.

In one region, school leaders gathered together by region to discuss leadership and effective implementation of regional policies. This positioned the leaders to build professional networks and gain immediate exposure to others, mutually building their regional leadership capacity (Scott & Rarieya, 2011).

Continuous/Current Professional Development (CPD) is a strategy that came from the proceedings of the International Conference on School Leader Preparation, Licensure/ Certification, Selection, Evaluation, and Professional Development (Lin, 2002). This process was piloted in South Africa where the public conversation shifted from questioning a leader's skills to emphasizing the importance of training a leader to develop needed skills.

There is a clear recognition that extensive teaching experience is no longer sufficient for school leaders (Van Der Westhuizen & Van Vuuren, 2007). Instead, CPD provides leaders with administrative and management skills to greatly enhance the quality of their work (Mestry, 2017). National education leaders have multiple options for developing leadership strategies among current school leaders, each of which prioritizes learning leadership skills relevant to the changing demands of East African school leaders.

As programs develop to support leaders currently assigned to schools, there must be equitable resources allocated to develop preparation programs to train candidates before they are appointed as school leaders. Research centered in African contexts demonstrated that preparation programs are quite useful for the success of school leaders (Webber et al., 2014). There is a growing recognition of a moral obligation to train school leaders (Bush, 2009). They have access to financial resources, they are responsible for human resources, and they greatly influence student success in schools.

Leaders must also become socialized to their new position through an examination of their professional and organizational roles in the context of a preparation program (Bush, 2009). This can also be accomplished through mentoring, a process that aligns a more experienced leader with a leader candidate to influence their understanding of the field (Onguko et al., 2008). Mentoring is particularly necessary when there is a lack of accessible preparation programs.

African education leadership preparation programs are generally located within university settings, often in urban areas (Onguko et al., 2008). All programs are face-to-face, without options for remote access or distance learning. This makes program accessibility challenging for many (Onguko et al., 2008). Based on the projected increase in the number of schools due to policy changes that require free education for all, there are not enough preparation programs to meet the projected needs of school leaders (Onguko et al., 2008).

Research conducted in Kenya identified key components of coursework included in preparation programs for school leaders (Asuga, Scevak, & Eacott, 2016). The researchers found a diverse set of course offerings, which are likely to prepare leaders for the contextual realities of leading a school in East Africa. Although another study found that most preparation program do not prioritize instructional leadership or technology (Onguko et al., 2008), it is clear that the program of study in Kenya is regarded as a strong regional option for leadership preparation.

From the International Study of Principal Preparation (ISPP) (www.Ucalgary.ca/ispp/) a study conducted in fourteen countries, researchers found that Kenya and Tanzania promoted core philosophical principles to frame their preparation programs. These included a recognition that education serves a civil society, is a basic right, and that leadership can be taught and nurtured to prioritize learning and promote inclusivity (Webber et al., 2014).

Based on the strength of select programs in several East African nations and the similarities of education across the region, cross-border leadership preparation options are strongly recommended for greater access to effective training (Onguko et al., 2008). Leadership preparation has an indigenous framework that is likely to generate a network of well-trained school leaders who can navigate success in an East African context.

African school leaders confirm that they would be more effective if they had training or other supports to strengthen their capacity as school leaders (Mestry, 2017). In their role as leaders, they described that the skills necessary to lead a school cannot be gained simply through an extensive career as a classroom teacher.

In order to create a lasting solution for schools across the region, national leaders need to consider changing the leadership promotion process to emphasize a search for qualified leaders rather than a search for the most experienced classroom teachers (Mestry, 2017). This type of change requires the professionalization of the school leader position in East Africa to disseminate leadership training to school leaders across the region. By training those currently installed and developing preparation programs for eligible candidates, with an attention to the contextual realities of the area, school leadership will become a profession that surpasses the expectations of those formerly identified as headteachers (Tigistu, 2013).

BACKGROUND—ETHIOPIA

Ethiopia, five times the size of the United Kingdom, is a large and a diverse country with a population of 102 million, with more than ninety ethnic and linguistic groups (World Bank, 2018). Since 1991, Ethiopia has changed its system of government from a centrally planned to a federal structure, establishing nine regional states and two autonomous city administrations.

Economically, Ethiopia aspires to be a lower-middle-income country by 2025, moving away from a state of widespread extreme poverty across rural and urban areas. This aspiration created micro-economic policy resulting in an impressive average annual growth of 10 percent over the last decades, compared to 5 percent for the region (Ministry of Education [MoE], 2015). Due to such sustained economic growth, the country has reduced extreme poverty from 39 percent in 2005 to 30 percent in 2010, achieved Under Five Mortality Rate (U5MR) of 88 per live birth, a 47 percent reduction from 2000, and increased the life expectancy at birth to almost sixty-five years (MoE, 2015).

Consistent with its economic growth and social transformation goals, Ethiopia made a strategic investment in its education sector. The Education and Training Policy (Transitional Government of Ethiopia [TGE], 1994), now under implementation through twenty years prospective Education Sector Development Program (ESDP I-V), created impressive progress in key education indicators.

For example, access to basic education increased from less than 22 percent in 1991 to 95 percent in 2013 (MoE, 2013); the gender gap in primary education narrowed from 30 percent ten years earlier to 6 percent in year 2010/2011 (MoE, 2013); and the educational disparity that existed between rural and urban, as well as central (relatively affluent) and emerging (disadvantaged), regions declined significantly over the last ten years. Reflecting this progress, the country has increased the number of schools from 11,000 in 1996 to 32,048 in 2014. The number of students also increased from 3 million to 18 million within the same time frame (MoE, 2015).

Despite the progress in expanding education access, meeting learning outcomes remains low and Ethiopia faces challenges in providing quality education for its citizens. As an example, student performance on national exams has never reached the government's 50 percent targets over the last two decades (MoE, 2013); even worse, there is a declining trend in student learning performance growth, particularly in disadvantaged regions of the country.

Such challenges in learning outcomes alarmed the government to initiate yet another policy, known as General Education Quality Improvement Reform (MoE, 2015), which included reforming the quality of school leadership as its major focus. As part of this effort, the MoE standardized leadership preparation by synchronizing the curriculum of all university-based programs, linking program elements to school improvement goals.

In tandem with national education reform efforts, the government of Ethiopia decentralized school leadership decisions to the local and regional authorities (Bush & Glover, 2016). This decision was enacted to promote decision-making through local councils and authorized national education administrators to set and evaluate education policy (Onguko et al., 2008).

Although hailed as empowering local leadership, it quickly became clear that without appropriate allocations of fiscal and human resources, local schools were simply unable to equip their leaders with the requisite tools for successful school leadership (Bush & Glover, 2016). In fact, two major concerns remain that render leadership preparation reform in Ethiopia as a missed opportunity to thoroughly address school improvement needs.

First, the fit between preparation and the roles of the principal's office is less known to policy makers charged with leadership development. The MoE involved experts and donor agencies as it designed the preparation model, importing best practices from other countries that support school improvement needs. However, experience suggests that "externally-driven models" are questionable to the unique work demands of principals in Africa (Eacott & Asuga, 2014; Smit, 2017).

As most school leaders in the sub-Saharan Africa, principals in Ethiopia encounter broad social justice issues on a daily basis that make their work exceedingly difficult. Some of these challenges include youth marriage and pregnancy, poor student personal hygiene, HIV/AIDS infections, child labor, and orphanage placement (Onguko et al., 2008); water sanitation (Poirier, 2012); parental illiteracy and low school participation (Swift-Morgan, 2006), among many others. Thus, it is difficult to determine how the preparation of school leaders fosters the capacity principals require as social justice leaders as they address these and many other unique contextual challenges.

Second, although the MoE's quality framework and standardization provide broad benchmarks defining the principals' roles, the decentralization of the education system means that the work demands of school leaders significantly varies by regions, zones, districts, and schools. In addition, regions vary in terms of resources, development levels, urbanization, socioeconomic activities, and cultural and population diversity. It is, thus, imperative to examine how the synchronization of courses and the curriculum allows principals to prepare for unique and diverse sets of social, cultural, and equity-related challenges and opportunities that occur in each school.

Across the continent of Africa, other nations have made similar assertions that the most expeditious route to education reform lies in improving, or in some instances establishing, leadership preparation programs for school leaders. There is an emerging recognition, rooted in Western scholarship, that school leaders play an essential role in increasing student achievement at the school level.

In West Africa, an educator was quoted, "There is a limited but growing realization that headship is a specialist role, not simply an extension of classroom teaching" (Bush & Glover, 2016). This reflects the understanding at the root of Ethiopia's leadership preparation goals; education reform will not be achieved by simply placing former teachers in leadership positions, but rather by developing preparation programs to position leaders to complete the work of school reform efforts.

PURPOSE AND METHODOLOGY

The data presented in this chapter is part of a larger, national study of school leadership and leadership development within Ethiopia. This study draws insight from experiential learning theory (Kolb, 2000) and situated cognition theory (Brown, Collins, & Duguid, 1989; Clancy, 1997). Experiential learning theory helps unpack how school leaders engage in new learning through concrete experiences, reflective observation, abstract conceptualization, and active experimentation (Kolb, 2000). Situated cognition theory helps understand how the design of leadership preparation is relevant and adaptable to the context in which it is used, linking preparation to principals' work demands (Brown et al., 1989; Clancy, 1997).

This study examined the fit between preparation and work demands of Ethiopian school leaders to understand how both the very conception of leadership and the way school leaders are prepared encapsulate culturally responsive practices and models of leadership development in Ethiopia.

Methodology included a narrative analysis of school principal interviews, content analysis of national education leadership policies, and an evaluation of preparation programs. Interviews with principals helped validate the information from document analysis as well as stimulated nuanced understanding of role expectations in the principal's office from an emic perspective. In other words, interviews helped unpack the unwritten and complex dimensions of the principal's roles that formal job descriptions tend to discount. All participant responses were translated from Amharic to English by the researchers.

The book chapter highlights the quest for innovative practices of Ethiopian school leaders to implement culturally responsive school leadership in a context challenged by globalization trends. This study utilizes an asset-driven approach to describe specific leader behaviors that disrupt national expectations of headteachers, establishing new expectations of professionalization that transforms the local context through social justice advocacy, and indigenous constructs and approaches to leadership development.

FINDINGS OF ETHIOPIAN LEADERSHIP PREPARATION

Ethiopia produced a national leadership and planning preparation program through a collaborative effort of field experts and leaders from international donor organizations (World Bank, 2008). Review of the policy and standards document (MoE, 2014) yielded confirmation that the MoE missed worthwhile opportunities to advance an indigenous study of school leadership practices necessary to achieve the national education reform goals. Rather than creating meaningful involvement for Ethiopian institutions of higher education, the Ministry utilized external resources with limited knowledge of indigenous contexts impacting daily leadership priorities of school principals and limited local scholarly involvement to ceremonial courtesies. This was evident through a cursory glance at the reading lists for the program, naming prominent Western scholars who contribute to Western systems of education leadership development.

In addition, learning objectives were supplanted from Western institutions of higher education, reflecting foreign concepts not situated in an Ethiopian setting. In doing so, the national leadership and planning preparation program neglected to adequately prepare Ethiopian leaders for the nuanced demands of their current school contexts. Additionally, these standards were centralized and failed to reflect the regional differences that impact schools across Ethiopia. The following section outlines two key themes that emerged from this study, referencing specific elements of Ethiopia's leadership preparation policy document.

Job Responsibility—Politics Comes First

Ethiopian school leaders were charged with the responsibility of responding to political demands from regional authorities that often disrupt their daily agendas and alter their immediate work priorities. Contrary to the goals of decentralization efforts, which sought to empower school leaders with local authority, several school leaders described the expectation that they must be immediately answerable to political decision-makers. A review of the national leadership preparation program reflected a portion of the program studies dedicated to leadership in education and one for policy in education.

In that section, the document listed one of its goals to "undertake a decentralized management of educational system in accordance with Ethiopian constitution and education laws" (MoE, 2014, p. 193).

Beyond this statement, there is no further guidance to support school leaders' understanding of how to satisfy both regional political demands and meet the immediate needs of the local school. In fact, the preparation program failed to articulate the authority granted to local school leaders in the face of regional policy makers, furthering inconsistent school leadership priorities and complicating principals' daily work agendas.

The recognition of the inconsistent directives of this policy document was informed by interviews with Ethiopian school leaders. One leader was asked specifically about instances where he may deviate from his daily work agenda or times when his work plan is rendered ineffective. The leader responded,

> Oh yes, there are many time-born/urgent activities that interfere with my routine and regular work as a principal. Sometimes I receive urgent instruction from the party office to which I cannot say no. Therefore, as much as I do not enjoy doing those sorts of things, I have no choice but to put my schoolwork on the side; when that happens, I delegate someone to carry out my school duties while I attend to the political call.

This reflected an implicit understanding among school principals that their leadership responsibilities include responding to regional party leaders, often without notice or consensual agenda-setting.

Principals were not just tasked with responding to education policy work, they were also asked to fulfill political goals outside the scope of education. The same leader shared an example of his involvement in political activities dictated by the government, tasks assigned to him through his school leadership role.

> As a principal I am involved in political campaigns and called away from my major in-school-roles to ensure successful implementation of the rural transformation program of the government which for example entails harvesting crops during untimely heavy rains or mobilizing parents to send their children to school when enrollments drops and so on. I would be disingenuous if I say there is no interference from the higher-ups. It happens all the time and at times, it may even render your plan and your job as a principal ineffective.

His comments advanced recognition that school principals constantly make political calculations when acting as school leaders, seeking to meet the political demands of regional authorities and address local concerns at their schools. They were ultimately required to increase student achievement, ensure consistent attendance, and advance reform efforts to improve school conditions in their local area. But leaders consistently shared that they were ill-prepared to balance political and professional responsibilities. This reflected a missed opportunity for Ethiopian school leadership preparation programs that could clearly articulate how leaders should prioritize political expectations with local school tasks to satisfy all regional and local stakeholders that influence a leader's success.

Job Responsibility—Social Justice Advocates

Ethiopian school leaders often worked in school communities subjected to abject poverty but still needed to meet the school attendance and student performance objectives established through the national school reform initiatives. The national leadership preparation program assigned aspiring leaders to complete a course titled "Schools in Society" with vague objectives like "establishing positive relationship with the community and the school environment" or "creating strong link between the school and the environment in which it operates" (MoE, 2014, p. 80). With only one assigned reading titled *School and Community in the Third World* (Sinclair & Lillis, 1980), published in 1980 in London, this course missed a unique opportunity to empower school leaders with knowledge and strategies necessary to address the impacts of poverty on their local school communities.

Social justice advocacy requires leaders to disrupt systems of inequality by addressing the myriad of needs necessary to achieve a quality of life and well-being. In an Ethiopian context, this requires obtaining funding to secure food, clothing, shelter, access to drinking water and health care, and other necessities for students and their families. Such extreme conditions are not reflected in school leadership tasks in most Western nations.

This disconnect was reflected in the leadership development programs that failed to give school leaders strategies to address these concerns. Without a national system of welfare assistance, school leaders who want to prioritize social justice advocacy were tasked with innovating their own local solutions to national crises, often by distributing school administration duties to others on staff. One leader shared,

> My work as human resource manager and leader entails a clear job specification and then follow-up everyone based on that specification. When everyone does the internal job of the school, I can put my energy and focus on the external relationship of the school. For example, I leverage my position to seek out funding for needy students from NGOs. There are many needy kids in my school who need financial support who cannot afford to buy clothes or even to get their daily meals.
>
> I will collect evidence/data about these kids from the district they live to justify using these evidence as I ask the NGOs to support them. These kids primarily need food and a place to stay prior to education; they cannot attend

class properly with an empty stomach. So, addressing their basic needs equals to removing the barriers for learning so, honestly speaking, although this is not part of my job description, I am personally invested in it. When teachers and other administrators focus on the internal job of the school, I can work on the external aspect at least two or three days a month.

His reflection showed two distinct leadership initiatives enacted in a local context. One was the practice of distributing administrative responsibilities to allocate time for addressing social justice work. The other was to approach international donor organizations to obtain daily necessities for students and their families. Neither of these tasks were adequately reflected in the national preparation program details.

School leaders often described their social justice work not only in terms of necessary efforts to meet national expectations of student attendance and performance but because the work was meaningful and impactful to the lives of children and their families. After a detailed review of Ethiopia's national preparation program, there were missed opportunities of communicating meaning and relevance in the work of a school principal. Rather than detailing the tasks of school administration, leadership preparation programs can create a culture of leadership that is rooted in service, community transformation, and building meaningful relationships with others. This comes forth through the remarks of the same principal when he said,

> My job is rewarding to me not because of the salary I make or the prestige that comes with it but because of the impact I believe I can make on the lives of many students. Let me give you an example. There was a student in my school who received the best score in the entire region on the national exam, and successfully admitted to the best medical school in the nation. He was a homeless child when I met with him and had a mother who lived in abject poverty and no father. As soon as I knew him, I worked out with a local NGO for help that allowed him to receive subsistence money for his food and lodging until he graduated from my high school. Then he had no money for transportation to the university. I had to buy him not only a bus ticket but also a laptop from my own personal money. I consider him as my own child. I am proud of him because he defied his background and entered the best medical school in the country. Therefore, the success of my students particularly someone like him inspires me every day.

Although school leaders around the globe often use their positions to serve local communities, this comment reflected a unique Ethiopian context of a leader who sought international funding, used personal resources, and addressed complicated needs of an individual child to ensure their access to school and future success. It was a missed opportunity for the preparation program in Ethiopia not to tell these stories of leadership success on a national level to promote the social justice work needed to transform local communities to places where children and their families can thrive.

CONCLUSION

Following the 1974 Education Training Policy (TGE, 1974), the government of Ethiopia created a decentralized educational structure that provided more autonomy for regional governments, districts, and local schools. The result of this reform is that the school leader's day-to-day management of schools is under the purview of regional governments, but policy remains a national initiative. The MoE continues to play a key role in the development of national education policies, relegating implementation to local and regional district leaders. This structure is problematic because it not only disrupts the essence of decentralization to empower local leaders to make autonomous decisions according to local contexts, but also it undermines school leaders' local priorities through implicit expectations to meet external political demands.

Another result of the decentralization process was the development of the national leadership preparation program. The MoE organized a single, national curriculum borrowing Western practices of school leadership with minimal reference to Ethiopian contexts. It enforced curriculum harmonization that required all universities to adopt the same set of courses, without adjustments for local priorities. In addition, the curriculum did not reflect the voices of local principals and the challenges and opportunities they experience on a daily basis.

In spite of the limitations of the leadership preparation program, the principals were able to re-invent the principalship locally. For example, they sought to distribute administration responsibilities across staff members to allocate their time to address social justice inequities present in their local communities. Despite the persistence of external political demands, they continued to struggle to maintain a professional balance to address their immediate daily agendas of school administration.

A leadership preparation program that considers the challenges, opportunities, pressures, and innovative practices of school principals along with regional university preparation programs is imperative to ensure successful school reform and facilitate the country's Millennium Development Goals.

REFERENCES

Asuga, G., Scevak, J., & Eacott, S. (2016). Bringing a "local" voice to a "universal" discourse: School leadership preparation and development in Kenya. *International*

Studies in Educational Administration (Commonwealth Council for Educational Administration & Management (CCEAM), 44(1), 25–39.

Brown, J., Collins, A., & Duguid, P. (1989). Situated cognition and the culture of learning. Educational Researcher, 18(1), 32–42.

Bush, T. (2009). Leadership development and school improvement: Contemporary issues in leadership development. Educational Review, 61(4), 375–389.

Bush, T., & Glover, D. (2009). Managing teaching and learning: A concept paper. MGSLG, Johannesburg, 4, 162–168.

Bush, T., & Glover, D. (2016). School leadership in West Africa: Findings from a systematic literature review. Africa Education Review, 13(3–4), 80–103.

Bush, T., Kiggundu, E., & Moorosi, P. (2011). Preparing new principals in South Africa: The ACE: School leadership programme. South African Journal of Education, 31(1), 31–43.

Bush, T., & Oduro, G. K. (2006). New principals in Africa: Preparation, induction and practice. Journal of Educational Administration, 44(4), 359–375.

Clancey, W. (1997). Situated cognition: On human knowledge and computer representations. New York, NY: Cambridge University Press.

Eacott, A., & Asuga, G. (2014). School leadership preparation and development in Africa: A critical insight. Educational Management Administration and Leadership, 42(6), 919–934.

Kolb, D. (2000). The process of experiential learning. Strategic learning in a knowledge economy (pp. 313–331).Woublurn, MA: Butterworth-Heinemann.

Li, P. P. (2012). Toward an integrative framework of indigenous research: The geocentric implications of Yin-Yang Balance. Asia Pacific Journal of Management, 29(4), 849–872.

Lin, N. (2002). Social capital: A theory of social structure and action (Vol. 19). New York, USA: Cambridge University Press.

Mestry, R. (2017). Empowering principals to lead and manage public schools effectively in the 21st century. South African Journal of Education, 37(1), 1–11.

Ministry of Education. (2008). General education quality improvement package (GEQIP). Addis Ababa, Ethiopia: Author. Retrieved from http://info.moe.gov.et/ggdocs/GEQIP_Plan.pdf

Ministry of Education. (2010). Education sector development program IV (ESDP IV): 2010/2011–2014/2015. Addis Ababa, Ethiopia: Author.

Ministry of Education. (2013). Education statistics annual abstract (2013/14). Addis Ababa, Ethiopia: Author.

Ministry of Education. (2014). National curriculum for MA degree in school leadership. Addis Ababa, Ethiopia: Author.

Ministry of Education. (2015). Education sector development program V (ESDP-V) 2015/16–2019/20. Program action plan. Addis Ababa, Ethiopia: Author. Retrieved from https://www.globalpartnership.org/content/education-sector-plan-2016-2020-ethiopia

Moloi, K., & Bush, T. (2006). An overview of education management in South Africa. Management in Education, 20(5), 15–22.

Onguko, B., Abdalla, M., & Webber, C. F. (2012). Walking in unfamiliar territory: Headteachers' preparation and first-year experiences in Tanzania. *Educational Administration Quarterly, 46*(6), 441–455.

Oplatka, I. (2004). The principalship in developing countries: Context, characteristics and reality. *Comparative Education, 40*(3), 427–448.

Poirier, T. (2012). The effects of armed conflict on schooling in sub-Saharan Africa. *International Journal of Educational Development, 32*(2), 341–351.

Scott, S., & Rarieya, J. F. (2011). Professional development of school leaders: Cross-cultural comparisons from Canada and East Africa. *International Studies in Educational Administration (Commonwealth Council for Educational Administration & Management [CCEAM]), 39*(1).

Sinclair, M. E., & Lillis, K. (1980). *School and community in the Third World*. London: Croom Helm.

Smit, B. (2017). A narrative inquiry into rural school leadership in South Africa. *Qualitative Research in Education, 6*, 1–21.

Sperandio, J., & Merab Kagoda, A. (2010). Women teachers' aspirations to school leadership in Uganda. *International Journal of Educational Management, 24*(1), 22–33.

Spring, J. (2001). *Globalization and educational rights: An intercivilizational analysis*. Mahwah, NJ: L. Erlbaum Associates.

Swift-Morgan, J. (2006). What community participation in schooling means: Insights from Southern Ethiopia. *Harvard Education Review, 76*(3), 339–367.

Tekleselassie, A. (2002). The deprofessionalisation of school principalship: Implications for reforming school leadership in Ethiopia. *International Studies in Educational Administration, 30*, 57–64.

Tigistu, K. (2013). Professionalism in early childhood education and care in Ethiopia: What are we talking about? *Childhood Education, 89*(3), 152–158.

Transitional Government of Ethiopia. (1994). *Education and training policy* (1st ed.). Addis Ababa, Ethiopia: St. George Printing Press.

Tsui, A. S. (2004). Contributing to global management knowledge: A case for high quality indigenous research. *Asia Pacific Journal of Management, 21*(4), 491–513.

United Nations, General Assembly. (2000). United Nations Millennium Declaration, A/55/L.2.

Van der Westhuizen, P., & Van Vuuren, H. (2007). Professionalising principalship in South Africa. *South African Journal of Education, 27*(3), 431–445.

Wamba, N. (2015). Headteacher preparation in Mzuzu, Malawi, Africa. *Journal of Education and Learning, 4*(4), 119.

Webber, C., Mentz, K., Scott, S., Mola Okoko, J., & Scott, D. (2014). Principal preparation in Kenya, South Africa, and Canada. *Journal of Organizational Change Management, 27*(3), 499–519.

Whetton, C. (2009). A brief history of a testing time: National curriculum assessment in England 1989–2008. *Educational Research, 51*(2), 137–159.

World Bank. (2018). *The World Bank in Ethiopia: Overview*. Retrieved from http://www.worldbank.org/en/country/ethiopia/overview

Young, M., Mountford, M., & Skrla, L. (2006). Infusing gender and diversity issues into educational leadership programs: Transformational learning and resistance. *Journal of Educational Administration, 44*(3), 264–277.

Chapter Four

Principals' Taking Initiative Level and School Circumstances in Turkey

Emine Babaoğlan

Organizations that encourage their staff to engage in self-starting behaviors and provide a personally nonthreatening work atmosphere are more likely to be successful in terms of organizational goal achievement. Process innovations should be accompanied by an atmosphere that allows for an active approach toward work and for interpersonal risk-taking to be successful (Baer & Frese, 2003).

Because of the increasing rates of innovation, global competition, and changes in the overall job market, tomorrow's jobs will require more personal initiative than exists within the contemporary world (Frese & Fay, 2001). Because more and more organizations, including educational institutions, are moving from traditional organizational structures to change-oriented institutions, for employees to support change processes effectively, manager (leader) should encourage and increase personal initiative (Baer & Frese, 2003; Frese, Garst, & Fay, 2007).

Taking initiative (readiness, ability to act) is a crucial element of leadership and an important asset for many jobs. In many respects, individual responsibilities are increased due to change. To keep pace with changing requirements, people must continue to develop their knowledge and skills. The change in the job concept makes it necessary for people to actively engage in continuous participation in the labor market. In today's organizations, employees must make decisions on their own, and they must follow through on these decisions (Frese & Fay, 2001).

Personal initiative is a behavior resulting both in an individual taking an active and self-starting approach to work and tasks, as well as persisting in dealing with barriers and setbacks, going beyond what is formally required in a given job. Personal initiative is characterized by organizational mission; long-term focus; goal direction and action-orientation; persistence in the face of difficulties, barriers, and setbacks; as well as self-starting and proactive behaviors (Frese, Fay, Hilburger, Leng, & Tag, 1997; Frese, Kring, Soose, & Zempel, 1996).

While pursuing new projects and goals, employees can experience problems, barriers, and setbacks. If an employee does not give up in the face of barriers, there is initiative. This implies that the employee deals with problems actively and persistently (Frese et al., 1996, 1997).

Personal initiative is determined according to the degree of psychological distance. If someone's proposal related to job is very similar to that of others, the psychological distance is low. On the other hand, if someone's proposal related to job is very different to that of others, the psychological distance is high (Frese & Fay, 2001).

If a manager (leader) follows a strategy that is clearly visible, promoted by other executives, or discussed in institutional publications, the psychological distance is small, and these actions are not considered to be personal initiative. If the strategy is suggested by subordinates, it implies a high psychological distance and is considered a personal initiative (Fay & Frese, 2001).

Likewise, if the manager (leader) assumes a strategy that is not known or is unusual for the organization, then this is psychologically high distance and it is considered that he/she is using personal initiative, which is a proactive process. This proactive approach involves trying to provide feedback, develop signals to indicate future problems, and develop plans to prevent these problems from becoming active (Fay & Frese, 2001).

Personal initiative needs to be self-starting, proactive, and persistent. *Self-starting* means that a person does something without explicit instruction or external pressure; it is not an explicit role requirement. Even though this is not part of one's job description, a person does something. Thus, personal initiative is the pursuit of self-set goals in contrast to assigned goals (Frese & Fay, 2001, Frese et al., 2007).

Personal initiative is a self-starting action that exceeds the work role. It often implies a certain rebellious element toward the supervisor. However, in the long run, personal initiative must be in accordance with overall organizational goals. Actions that lack a pro-company orientation are not personal initiative (Fay & Frese, 2001).

Proactivity means to have a long-term focus and not waiting until one must respond to a demand. The long-term focus on work allows the individual to consider future concerns, such as new demands, new or recurrent problems, or emerging opportunities. The individual then initiates an action without prompting from others. Thus, when problems and opportunities arise, the person is ready to deal with them in a timely, efficient, and effective manner (Frese & Fay, 2001; Frese et al., 2007).

Persistence is defined as firm or obstinate continuance in a course of action in spite of difficulty or opposition (Google Translate, n.d.). In general, personal initiative implies that something has changed: a process, a procedure, or a task has been added or changed. The changes usually do not work perfectly at first; they may even become a failure. People affected by the changes may not like having to adapt to something new and changing their routines. Thus, persistence is critical as organizations and individuals attempt to initiate change, as well as overcome the resistance and inertia of other people (Frese & Fay, 2001; Frese et al., 2007).

Implementation of long-term goals often leads to similar problems and barriers. Because new proposal for work improvement or new procedures to do things may not have been tried before, people within the organization will likely experience difficulties (Fay & Frese, 2001). Individuals with high personal initiative seem to actively attack a problem, and thus seem to be willing to face and overcome problems and corresponding barriers. Personal initiative seems to serve as a motivational promoter and makes it more likely that an individual engages in working on a creative solution (Binnewies, Ohly, & Sonnentag, 2007).

Furthermore, individuals with high personal initiative are goal oriented and strive to achieve a creative outcome. More engagement in creative sub-processes also implies spending more time working on the creative solution. Because people who are high in personal initiative are more likely to be goal oriented and more focused on having a creative and positive outcome, they might not be willing to spend as much time in the creative process but might want to just put the idea into practice. Such people might also achieve higher idea creativity by identifying more important problem areas (Binnewies et al., 2007).

There have been few researches in Turkey about taking initiative (Akın & Anlı, 2011; Cereci, 2018; Gündüz, Çakmak & Korumaz, 2015; Gündüz & Hamedoğlu, 2012; Nayır & Taşkın, 2017). One of the first studies on initiative was the study conducted by Akın and Anlı (2011), which investigated the validity and reliability of the Turkish version of the Personal Growth Initiative Scale. Personal Growth Initiative Scale was found positively related to self-kindness, awareness of common humanity, and mindfulness.

In Çelebi, Güner, and Yıldız's (2015) research, it was found that factors such as teacher motivation; successful, harmonious environment; and sense of belonging are closely related to the leadership behavior of the principals. In addition, negative principal behaviors affect school climate and school culture, job satisfaction, and organizational effectiveness.

Another study on initiative in Turkey was Nayır and Taşkın's (2017) research, which was to identify the relationship between the perceived organizational support of teachers and their initiative behaviors. Findings suggested that there was a low-level relationship between perceived organizational support and initiative-taking behaviors; gender, marital status, branch, seniority, and school-type variables generated significant differences on initiatives behavior.

The study being presented in this chapter is unique because it examines a relatively new concept in Turkey. Turkey is governed by educational organizations' centralized management approach. According to Güven, Karkacıer, and Şimşek (2017), the central government is about the taking of general decisions from a single center of the country in order to protect the sovereignty of the states. According to administering duties centrally and distributing and using available resources more effectively and efficiently for the people's benefit as a whole; however centralization has limitations as well (Oktay, 2013).

Making leadership, to take initiative without waiting for instruction from anyone, is to show the ability to make decisions. Using the initiative means not to follow the rules, but to sense exceptional circumstances that will break these rules (Aksoy, 2011).

Since the general decisions are taken by the central manager (leader), the school principals' decision of the school administrators is limited. In centralized management, by making decisions school administrators adhere to the centralized decisions. For this reason, principals are limited in their decision-making process. In the research, Kıral and Nacak (2018) found that according to the school administrators, the main obstacle to the development of the school's leadership capacity is the restrictions on regulations.

School administrators have a number of responsibilities, even if which are not in the legislation, such as financial and extracurricular activities. School managers have to undertake responsibilities such as; "funding/raising funds" in terms of financial affairs; "to do the paint/repair works of the school building" in terms of human resources affairs; "having to deal with parental problems" in terms of student affairs (Cereci, 2018). In Babaoğlan, Nalbant, and Çelik's (2017) research, it was determined that the ideal manager should take risk and be an entrepreneur.

While some schools in Turkey continue to function routinely, others work beyond what is expected to enhance the opportunities to be successful. One of the biggest reasons that may account for the different practices in these schools is the initiative-taking behavior of teachers and administrators. The following major question guided the study: What is the school environment in Turkey for principals taking initiative?

In addition, the study attempted to answer the following questions:

1. What is the level of school principals taking initiative?
2. Which environments-circumstances allow the school principals to express their views?

3. In what kind of environments did school principals express their opinions comfortably?
4. Were/are the school principals' proposals often presented by their colleagues or not?
5. Did/do the school principals present additional (extraordinary/exceptional) energy or new ideas that went beyond expected behavior in their job?

METHODOLOGY

Study Group

This research was descriptive and qualitative. In this study, 20 school managers (leader) were interviewed; 11 of these participants were school principals and 9 were vice-principals. Three of the participants were female. School managers (leaders) first were asked about their personal and professional characteristics (gender, age, number of children, type of program they graduated from, position, school type, year of work, and duration of management). Personal and professional characteristics of the participants are seen in table 4.1.

The participants were determined with snowball sampling (Yıldırım & Şimşek, 2000). The snowball sampling is one of the purposeful sampling methods. In the interview process, firstly an administrator was contacted and interviewed. The interviewee was asked to advise new managers to interview. Thus, the sample was expanded by taking new manager names from each interviewed manager.

Interview Questions

Face-to-face interviews were conducted by the researcher with the participants during the data collection process. Four open-ended questions about the general initiative were asked to the participants. In this research, four open-ended questions were asked to the participants. Open-ended questions were based on Fay and Frese's (2001) research questions. The four questions were as follows:

1. During the last two years/or now, did you submit proposals to improve work? Please give two examples. (self-starting)
   If yes:
2.a. Which environments-circumstances allow you to express your views?
   If no:
2.b. In what kind of environments-circumstances did you express your opinions comfortably? Please give two examples.
   If yes:

Table 4.1 Personal and professional characteristics of the participants

	Gender	Age	Children (n)	Graduation	Position	School type	Educational experience (years)	Educational management experience (years)
1	Male	51	2	Education faculty	Principal	High school	27	20
2	Male	45	2	Education faculty	Principal	Primary and secondary	23	16
3	Female	50	-	Master	Vice-principal	High school	25	22
4	Male	43	3	Education faculty	Principal	Primary and secondary	21	4
5	Male	50	2	Education faculty	Vice-principal	Primary school	27	11
6	Male	47	3	Education faculty	Principal	Primary school	25	15
7	Male	34	1	Education faculty	Vice-principal	Primary and secondary	11	10
8	Male	57	3	Education institute	Principal	Primary and secondary	38	20
9	Male	60	3	2 years education school	Principal	Secondary school	38	25
10	Male	47	3	Master	Principal	Secondary school	25	15
11	Male	38	2	Master	Principal	Primary school	14	14
12	Male	48	3	Faculty	Vice-principal	Primary school	27	10
13	Male	55	3	Education institute	Principal	Primary school	30	-
14	Male	60	2	Education institute	Vice-principal	Primary school	36	13
15	Male	32	1	Education faculty (continuing Master)	Vice-principal	Primary and secondary	12	4
16	Male	39	2	Faculty of theology	Principal	Primary and secondary school	14	10
17	Male	36	1	Education faculty	Vice-principal	Primary school	13	10
18	Male	39	2	Education faculty	Vice-principal	Primary school	17	10
19	Female	29	1	Education Faculty	Principal	High school	6	1
20	Male	47	2	Education faculty	Vice-principal	Middle school	24	14

3. Were/are your suggestions often presented by colleagues or not? (p*sychological distance*)
4. Do/did you present extra energy or new ideas that went/go beyond expected behavior in this job? Please give two examples.

Content Analysis

The research data were analyzed with content analysis. The data for each principal were coded as P1, P2, P3 . . . . P20. Principals' expressions were coded according to their contents. Frequency was determined according to the frequency of repetition of the coded statements. Frequency analysis is to reveal the frequency of the expressions. This type of analysis is to understand the intensity and importance of a particular statement (Tavşancıl & Aslan, 2000). Participant statements are expressed according to their frequency in the tables (Bilgin, 2006).

Validity and Reliability

During the preparation of the research questions, three interviewees were interviewed in order to ensure the reliability and validity of the interview questions. Questions were examined for clarity and suitability for research purpose. Questions were asked to the principals as they were written on the interview form, so that the same question was asked to all participants to provide the validity of the research (Yıldırım & Şimşek, 2000). To ensure the validity of the content analysis in the analysis process, content analysis was repeated in different times to ensure time triangulation (Cohen, Manion, & Morrison, 2005).

Data triangulation was performed by the participants to ensure that the collected data is valid. For this purpose, when the study group was determined, both male and female managers (leaders) working in different schools in Yozgat were preferred for interview, so the triangulation and sampling of the place is done (Gray, Williamson, Karp, & Dalphin, 2007). And also, the research steps have been detailed in order to allow the research to be repeated in the same way (Yıldırım & Şimşek, 2000) and to be able to demonstrate its reliability through transparency (Rubin & Rubin, 2005).

FINDINGS

In the research, the findings were presented in four themes. These themes were determined according to the interview questions. The participants' answers to the first question emerged as the first theme. In the same way, the answers of the participants to the second question formed second theme, the answers to the third question showed up third theme, and finally fourth question's answers created fourth theme. These themes are as follows:

- Theme 1. Offering proposal (self-starting)
- Theme 2. Circumstances allowing expression of views comfortably
- Theme 3. Similarity or dissimilarity of proposals (Theme 3: Psychological distance)
- Theme 4. Exerting extra energy or offering new ideas

Theme 1. Offering Proposal (Self-Starting)

Participant answers for the first theme were yes or no. These participant answers are shown in table 4.2.

The number of managers (leaders) who said they offered proposals to improve the work was 16, while the number of managers (leaders) who said they did not offer was 4. School principals' proposals are mostly helpful to the development of the school, manager (leader), students, teachers, and parents. One technical high school principal's proposal about teaching program was:

> School programs have changed frequently. I suggested that it should not change very often. So, I suggested that it is wrong to put the new program into practice without completely getting the results of an applied program and without applying it completely, enough time is needed to see the superior and incomplete aspects of the applied program.
>
> (P1)

Another elementary principal's proposal about teacher development was:

> I proposed that seminars and conferences should be conducted for the professional development of the teachers in the school. And we implemented my proposal.
>
> (P4)

A primary school vice-principal's proposal about teachers' opinions regarding to the teachers' *expectations from management was*:

> We suggested applying questionnaires to determine the level of satisfaction from manager (leader) and the shortcomings of the administrators in the school

Table 4.2 Offering proposal (self-starting)

Self-starting	n
P1, P2, P3, P4, P6, P7, P8, P9, P10, P11, P13, P15, P16, P17, P18, P20	16
P5, P12, P14, P19	4
Total	20

and the situations that teachers think should be in the manager (leader). We analyzed and evaluated the answers of questionnaire.

(P5)

An elementary school offered the following regarding school management and school budget:

I suggested that the school administrators split into two parts. The first should be the school director. The school principal is the person who makes the salary and payments, which improves the physical conditions of the school. Secondly, the head teacher should be responsible for teaching affairs. The head teacher is the person who prepares the project and raises the teachers to increase the quality of education in the school.

(P6)

One elementary vice-principal's proposals about teachers' salary was:

Salary and tuition fees should be re-arranged considering the place of duty of the teachers. Educators working in the West and East regions must get (take) different salary. In the East and South-East, the task should be more attractive. Teachers should stay in the East and South-East (underdeveloped regions of Turkey) and be encouraged to serve for a long time.

(P7)

One elementary vice-principal's proposals about teachers' rest in summer vacation was:

Summer camps should be organized so that teachers can get rid of the stress and exhaustion they spend especially during the course work. Existing teacher camps should be developed.

(P7)

Another primary school principal's proposals about what teachers should do:

I especially wanted that our first grade teachers should do at least one activity each year with their students. If they are done, in the future, children will be able to direct their teachers about determining which activities will be done. In this way, students socialize, become liberated; children can search for their own rights.

(P8)

An elementary school principal's proposal was:

I suggested that a counselor should be appointed for every five students to improve the quality of education. I advised the counselor to guide these students to the lesson success and personal issues. P9-I suggested that groups of mass-mailing messages be created to develop student, parent, and teacher relationships.

(P9)

One school principal's proposal about principal training was:

I emphasized the fact that school administrators should have pre-service principal education and this training should sometimes be repeated in-service. And also, I offered that school principals should be appointed according to merit system.

(P10)

The recommendation of a director about the managers to attend the seminar is as follows:

It is wrong that the same principals are always going to the seminars (in-service training) about the school administration. I suggested that the principals who will go to the seminar should be determined objectively. And, I offered top managers (leaders) don't distinguish among schools and managers (leaders). They should treat all schools and administrators equally.

(P13)

One vice-principal's recommendations about school inspectors and students' school absenteeism were as follows:

Until five or six years ago, schools were inspected by inspectors. Later, these controls were removed. I offered that these inspections should continue. These controls were very useful. We learn from inspection that our right knowledge is sometimes wrong. Sometimes there are things we do not see, and we are aware of them thanks to the inspection—control. We are aware of our shortcomings and are trying to complete our shortcomings thanks to the supervision by outside officers.

(P16)

According to the Ministry of National Education Regulation (Rules) for Secondary Education Institutions, every student has 20 days disabled (excused) and 10 days non-excused (without excuse) absenteeism. I think it's wrong to have a 10-day absence without excuse. The principal (main) task of the student is to continue the school. The student should be able to use absenteeism only because of his excuse. P16.

Two vice-principals' proposals about the charming school for students were:

I have tried to create a more peaceful and more interesting school for students, teachers and parents. I decorated school walls with cartoon characters that kids loved. So, I aimed those students to love school.

(P18)

Theme 2. Circumstances Allowing Expression of Views Comfortably

The circumstances allowing school principals and school vice-principals to express their views freely are seen in table 4.3.

According to findings, nine of twenty administrators stated that they expressed their opinions in reliable environments. Six managers (leaders) said that they express their views in every environment, four of them stated democratic environment, three of them said positive environment, and three of them said when the manager (leader) is respectful to the views, three of

Table 4.3 Circumstances allowing expression of views comfortably

	Environments-circumstances allow school principals and school vice-principals to express their views freely	n
1	In trustful environments P1, P3, P8, P10, P12, P13, P18, P19, P20	9
2	I express in every environment P4, P6, P7, P8, P13, P20	6
3	I express in a democratic environment P3, P10, P12, P19	4
4	When administrator is constructive (positive) P3, P8, P17	3
5	When the manager (leader) is respectful to the views—when they value view P3, P2, P18	3
6	In meetings P9, P16, P20	3
7	In virtual environments P9, P11, P16	3
8	When the manager (leader) is experienced P3, P8	2
9	When the manager (leader) is neutral P3, P8	2
10	Where meetings are held in response to questions P7, P20	2
11	When there are skilled manager (leader) P8, P10	2
12	In environments with mutual exchange of ideas P5, P13	2
13	When management open to development and change P3	1
14	In case management is rational P3	1
15	When the manager (leader) is not prejudiced P3	1
16	When manager (leader) shares P3	1
17	When there is a manager (leader) with consistent personality P3	1
18	Because we can be more relaxed than before P7	1
19	Because we can access our administrators more easily P7	1
20	In stress-free environments P18	1
21	Where academic information is shared P10	1
22	In the environment where scientific information is referenced P10	1
23	In seminars and courses P16	1
24	In official correspondence P16	1
25	When stakeholders' attitudes are positive P17	1
26	If the level of understanding of the people in the environment is high P12	1
27	In the absence of political oppression (pressure) P12	1
28	In environments where working conditions are better 18	1
	Total	57

them said they express their views in meetings. Some administrators have expressed trustful environments in the following words:

> I present my opinions when the manager (leader) is respectful and does not criticize the recommendation.
>
> (P3)

> If there is no penalty for proposal (criticism).
>
> (P12)

> I tell my suggestion in environments where there are good colleagues.
>
> (P18)

The school administrators expressed their views and suggestions mostly in a democratic-trustful environment; the administrator was open to criticism and the administrator was positive in manner. The directors have indicated 28 different items for which environments-circumstances allow them to express their views. These items have been repeated 57 times.

Theme 3. Similarity or Dissimilarity of Proposals (Theme 3: Psychological Distance)

The opinions from the sample of principals regarding the third theme are found in table 4.4.

It can be seen in table 4.4, most of school managers' (leaders') proposals are similar. It means that school managers' (leaders') proposals are not very different from one another. Only five of manager (leader) suggestions were different from others. According to these findings, psychological distance is small, and proposals are mostly similar.

Table 4.4 Similarity or dissimilarity of proposals

	Were/are your suggestions often presented by colleagues or not?	n
1	Similar suggestions P2, P4, P7, P12, P14, P17, P18, P19	8
2	Sometimes similar sometimes different suggestions P1, P6, P10, P13, P16, P20	6
3	Different suggestions P3, P9, P11, P15	4
4	My proposals are different for older people, but younger ones see more normal P8	1
5	No suggestion P5	1
	Total	20

Table 4.5 Exerting extra energy or offering new ideas

	Exerting extra energy or offering new ideas	n
1	Yes, I do more than I expected P3, P4, P6, P7, P8, P9, P11, P15, P16, P17, P19, P20	12
2	Sometimes P1, P10, P12, P13,	4
3	No P2, P5, P14, P18,	4
	Total	20

Theme 4. Exerting extra energy or offering new ideas

This theme explains how each manager performs extra work in addition to his or her job.

Twelve of the school administrators reported that they were working more than they expected, four reported that they were working sometimes more than they expected at school. Only four administrators reported that they were not working more than they expected at school. For example, one vice-principal stated,

> I can do more than I am expected from my work says this: I am doing additional work to strengthen the relationships between students and employees. I also started a traditional youth festival to create school culture.
>
> (P3)

Another proposed,

> I do not limit myself to what I must do. I always try to make the environment I am in better. My working hours are not limited to compulsory working hours. I also work outside of office hours. Apart from office hours, I also work for school.
>
> (P6)

Another elementary school principal said,

> I waive my private life if necessary, to do what expected best I can. I want to deserve my salary. I would like to be a staff worthy of my state and my nation (people) that brought me this day. I work to support the rulers of the country. I act with the belief that the country is the most loving and best in its duty.
>
> (P7)

Yet another primary school principal stated,

> Every day I come to school earlier than every person, and I go out from school later than every employee. The reason to come early is not to monitor or supervise employees. The reason for my early arrival at the school is that the school is

ready for teaching and it is not a problem in the school. When the school starts, if I am not there, the employees may think that the school has a problem and there is no principal. I saw success when I treated employees friendly.

(P8)

One elementary school vice-principal says that he does extra work for the school indicated:

I do extra work for the school, I work outside of the compulsory work hours, at least I must work at home 2–3 times in a month, sometimes I must go to school on the weekend. For example, I do things like the exam work, the school placement, the course application that our students or their parents must do. I will work in all matters if I know like repair work, computer malfunction, paint, etc., in school. I do not mind using my car for school work.

(P15)

One high school principal explains that he is working extra for his job:

I love doing my job and task. I see my school as my second home. I am happy to be in school and serve for the school. I do not act with the intention of filling a day or a period with a classical point of view. I want to change something until the end of duration of work as principal.

(P16)

One vocational high school vice-principal who has worked more than necessary explained like this:

As the school's governing team, we always aim one step further and always do think about what we can do better for school. We organize student events on the city center-square and try to promote the school's name and vocational education. This year we did the April 23 children festival, March 21 spring festival, and Arabaşı (food) festival.

(P19)

RESULTS AND DISCUSSION

Theme 1. Offering Proposal (Self-Starting)

According to principals' and vice-principals' views, most of the school managers (leaders) in this research offered proposals to improve their work. However, it can be said that the recommendations are not original and there are no proposals to solve the problems. It can be said that these proposals create the perception of fulfilling their responsibilities, but they are ineffective. In this theme, school manager (leader) taking initiative level is very small.

The findings of this study are similar to those of Nayır and Taşkın's (2017) research findings, which were found that teachers' taking initiative level is medium level.

Due to the large number of students, dual teaching (double shift schooling) is being done in Turkey schools. For this reason, school managers (leaders) arrive to school very early in the morning and leave very late; working time is prolonged. According to Aybek (2017), work is often carried out beyond working hours and school manager's (leader's) workload is increased. It can be said that in this research, school managers' (leaders') work intensity can also negatively affect taking initiative of manager (leader).

There is also a central management structure in Turkey. As a result, managers (leaders) have more responsibilities and their authority is more limited. If there were no central government and the manager (leader) had more authority, it could be said that the directors would take more initiative (Anbarlı Bozatay, 2016; Berkün, 2017) than the current one.

In the globalization process, education has ceased to be an epistemic process of production and sharing. Education is now seen as an economic parameter. Schools as a commercial enterprise; information, as sold commodity; education managers have been accepted as commercial operators. Company universities constitute the beginning of this development. In the near future, training managers will act as a company manager; they will be trained and tasked to plan and coordinate the form of training for work and production (Çelik, 2018a).

Small bureaucrats were not trained to reveal major, paradigmatic changes. Great mentalities, perspectives and cognitive processes are not appropriate to reveal the paradigm shifts. They are effective in revealing small changes and processes. Such proposals for change cannot come out of the general assumptions of the prevailing conception (Çelik, 2018b).

Theme 2. Circumstances Allowing Expression of Views Comfortably

According to administrators' opinions, they can mostly express their proposals in trustful environments. And then consecutively, the administrators express their opinions in democratic environments, when the upper manager (leader) was respectful to the suggestions, when the administrator has a positive attitude, in virtual environments, when the leader is experienced and neutral, where meetings are held in question and answer, and when there are skilled managers (leaders), and in environments with mutual exchange of ideas. It can be said that if the school administrators feel safe and comfortable themselves, they can express their suggestions freely.

Principals and vice-principals expressed their suggestions when leader was open to development; the leader was rational, not prejudiced, sharing, consistent, and understanding. And also, leaders expressed their opinions in stress-free environments, where academic information is shared, in the environment where scientific information is referenced, in seminars and courses, in official correspondence, when stakeholders' attitudes were positive, in the absence of political oppression or pressure, and in environments where working conditions are better.

According to Çelebi and Bayhan's (2008) research results, the school principals have potential creativities, and they use this capability in a positive way. However, in this study, as an important feature, it was considered that potential creativity of principals, who work in low social-economic schools, was low and the environment of the school was found to be an important factor in determining creativity of principals.

Theme 3. Similarity or Dissimilarity of Suggestions (Theme 3: Psychological Distance)

According to findings, most of school managers' (leaders') suggestions were similar. It means that school managers' (leaders') suggestions are not very different from one another and the psychological distance is small. It means that, according to the findings, school administrators' suggestions are not extraordinary. It can be said that the recommendations are repetition and the applicability is low. Also, it means that the recommendations of the manager (leader) do not include taking initiative. In another word, taking initiative level of managers' (leaders') suggestions is low.

It is necessary to think creatively in order to make original and unusual suggestions. Creativity requires being able to go out of the frame, and creativity makes it easy to take initiative (Salı, 2015, 2019; Salı & Köksal Akyol, 2015). Managers have to think creatively to make original and unusual suggestions.

Theme 4. Exerting Extra Energy or Recommending New Ideas

Most of the school administrators are working and offering suggestions more than they are expected in their work. According to the results, surely school leaders work long hours and make big efforts for their school. However, it is seen that the proposals and efforts do not produce a rooted solution to the problems and they involve superficial efforts. But it can be said that the efforts for suggestions are useless efforts to carry out the procedures, which are inconclusive, inefficient, and increase the workload. These findings are consistent with Cereci's (2018) findings that school administrators undertake additional responsibilities.

According to Gökçe and Şahin (2002), since the effectiveness of applications is not queried, works do not reach the result and the studies are only for the purpose of fulfilling the procedures. Turkey is also enhancing an existing application and paperwork in an inefficient operation of public institutions. In this context, for the effectiveness of education, a monitoring and evaluation system should be established within the Ministry of Education, the quality of education should be improved, and education should be improved in Turkey (Kavak, 2011).

As a result of this research, it is suggested that school principals and vice-principals are offering suggestions for develop their work; but their suggestions are not effective enough. Secondly, school principals recommend only trusty environments. Thirdly, their suggestions are similar and they are not extra ordinary. Fourthly, they present extra energy and new idea but their efforts and new ideas are not effective enough. Based on all these results, it can be said that school principals' and vice-principals' taking initiative level is low.

All employees need trusty and fair environments to offer their suggestions freely. For this reason, as Akkol (2016) states it, to realize the practices that regress justice in society and all implementations in education society must be trusty and fair. Education manager (leader) should act in accordance with ethical principles in their practice and ethical leadership in society (Akbaba Altun, 2003). In future research, the relationship between taking initiative and perception of trust can be investigated. In addition, it can be recommended to investigate the effectiveness of the taking initiative of school manager (leader).

REFERENCES

Akbaba Altun, S. (2003). Educational administration and values. *Journal of Values Education, 1*(1), 7–17.

Akın, A., & Anlı, G. (2011). Adaptation of individual development initiative scale to Turkish: Validity and reliability study. *Mersin University Education Faculty Journal, 7*(1), 42–49.

Akkol, M. L. (2016). The concept of social justice in music education. *The Journal of Abant İzzet Baysal University Education Faculty, 16*(İpekyolu Special Issue), 2153–2164.

Aksoy, T. (2011). *To produce tasks from the situation.* Retrieved from https://www.temelaksoy.com/durumdan-vazife-cikarmak/

Anbarlı Bozatay, Ş. (2016). A legislative arrangement that focused on the debates of centralized administration—decentralization: evaluations about law no 6360. *Çankırı Karatekin University Journal of Faculty of Economics and Administrative Sciences, 6*(1), 609–637.

Aybek, Ş. (2017). *Full day education every aspect. 19 April 2017.* Retrieved from http://www.egitimajansi.com/sahin-aybek/her-yonuyle-tam-gun-egitim-kose-yazisi-856y.html

Babaoğlan, E., Nalbant, A., & Çelik, E. (2017). Teacher opinions about the impact of the school principal on school success. *Mehmet Akif Ersoy University Journal, 43*, 93–109.

Baer, M., & Frese, M. (2003). Innovation is not enough: climates for initiative and psychological safety, process innovations, and firm performance. *Journal of Organizational Behavior, 24*, 45–68.

Berkün, S. (2017). Administration in terms of public. *Journal of Labor and Society, 6*(16), 638–663.

Bilgin, N. (2006). *Content analysis techniques and case studies in social sciences.* Ankara: Siyasal Publisher.

Binnewies, C., Ohly, S., & Sonnentag, S. (2007). Taking personal initiative and communicating about ideas: What is important for the creative process and for idea creativity? *European Journal Work and Organizational Psychology, 16*(4), 432–455.

Çelebi, N., & Bayhan, G. (2008). Evaluation of potential creativity level of school principals according to teachers' perception who work in primary education. *Education and Science Journal, 27*, 79–97.

Çelebi, N., Güner, H., & Yıldız, V. (2015). Developing toxic leadership scale. *Bartın University Journal of Education, 4*(1), 249–268.

Çelik, E. (2018a). Economic globalization and education. In: T. Erdoğan (Ed.), *Academic research in social, human and administrative sciences 6* (pp. 175–196). Ankara, Turkey: Gece Kitaplığı Publications.

Çelik, E. (2018b). Education and society. In: D. A. Arslan & G. Arslan (Eds.), *Sociology* (pp. 177–195). Mersin, Turkey: Paradigma Academy Publication.

Cereci, C. (2018). Additional responsibilities have to be undertaken by school administrators, even if not in the legislation. *Journal of Contemporary Administrative Science, 5*(2), 119–127.

Cohen, L., Manion, L., & Morrison, K. (2005). *Research methods in education* (5th ed.). London: Taylor & Francis.

Fay, D., & Frese, M. (2001). The concept of personal initiative: An overview of validity studies. *Human Performance, 14*(1), 97–124.

Frese, M., & Fay, D. (2001). Personal initiative: An active performance concept for work in the 21st century. *Research in Organizational Behavior, 23*, 133–187.

Frese, M., Fay, D., Hilburger, T., Leng, K., & Tag, A. (1997). The concept of personal initiative: Operationalization. *Journal of Occupational and Organizational Psychology, 70*(2), 139–161.

Frese, M., Garst, H., & Fay, D. (2007). Making things happen: Reciprocal relationships between work characteristics and personal initiative in a four-wave longitudinal structural equation model. *Journal of Applied Psychology, 92*(4), 1084–1102.

Frese, M., Kring, W., Soose, A., & Zempel, J. (1996). Personal initiative at work: Differences between East and West Germany. *Academy of Management Journal, 39*(1), 37–63.

Gökçe, O., & Şahin, A. (2002). Problems of Turk bureaucracy in the 21st Century and suggestions for solutions. *Selçuk Üniversitesi İktisadi ve İdari Bilimler Fakültesi Sosyal ve Ekonomi Araştırmalar Dergisi, 2*(3), 1–27.

Google Translate. (n.d.). *Persistence.* Retrieved from https://translate.google.com/#view=home&op=translate&sl=en&tl=tr&text=persistence

Gray, P. S., Williamson, J. B., Karp, D. A., & Dalphin, J. R. (2007). *The research imagination: An introduction to qualitative and quantitative methods*. Cambridge, United Kingdom: Cambridge University Press.

Gündüz, H. B., Çakmak. E., & Korumaz, M. (2015). Taking initiative in educational organizations: A scale development study. *International Journal of Human Sciences, 12*(2), 327–342.

Gündüz, H. B., & Hamedoğlu, M. A. (2012). *The level of initiative taking of school administrators*. 6th National Education Management Congress, Malatya.

Güven, A., Karkacıer, A., & Şimşek, T. (2017). Problem of guardianship control in local administrations within the context of centralization localization discussions. *Journal of Information Economics and Management, 12*(2), 189–208.

Kavak, Y. (2011). Population and education in Turkey: Long-term (2010–2050) population projections and reflections on the education system. *The Journal of National Education, 192*, 86–105.

Kıral, E., & Nacak, H. (2018). The opinions of the administrator and teachers on school's leadership capacity. *EYFOR Conference Proceedings book* (pp. 1742–1771). Ankara: Eyuder Publishing.

Nartgün, Ş. S., & Taşkın, S. (2017). Relationship between teacher views on levels of organizational support—Organizational identification and climate of initiative. *Universal Journal of Educational Research, 5*(11), 1940–1954.

Nayır, F., & Taşkın, P. (2017). The relationship between perceived organizational support and taking initiative behavior in educational organizations. *YYU Journal of Education Faculty, 14*(1), 1319–1356.

Oktay, A. (2013). Decentralization in—and of—education. *Procedia—Social and Behavioral Sciences, 106*, 777–782.

Patton, M. Q. (1987). *How to use qualitative methods in evaluation Program evaluation kit* (2nd ed.). California: SAGE.

Rubin, H. J., & Rubin, I. S. (2005). *Qualitative interviewing: The art of hearing data*. California: Thousand Oaks, Sage Publication.

Salı, G. (2015). A longitudinal study on the development of creativity in children. *The Anthropologist, 20*(1,2), 93–100.

Salı, G. (2019). Teachers' creativity and empathic tendencies. *Kastamonu Education Journal*, in press.

Salı, G., & Köksal Akyol, A. (2015). Study on the creativity of preschool and elementary school teachers and their students. *Perceptual and Motor Skills, 121*(3), 1–9.

Tavşancıl, ve Aslan, E. (2001). *Content analysis and application examples for verbal, written and other materials*. İstanbul: Epsilon Publishing.

Yıldırım, A., & Şimşek, H. (2000). *Qualitative research methods in the social sciences* (2nd ed.). Ankara, Turkey: Seçkin Publishing.

About the Authors

Emine Babaoğlan is professor of educational administration and leadership at Yozgat Bozok University in Yozgat, Türkiye. Her scholarly interests include gender in school leadership, and she is the author of numerous scholarly articles. She has been the chief editor of the *Journal of Contemporary Administrative Science* since 2014.

Amaarah Decuir is a professorial lecturer at American University's School of Education. Her research appears in several peer-reviewed journals including *Journal of Education Administration and History* and the *International Journal for Education Leadership and Preparation*. Her work is informed by over 20 years of school leadership and classroom-teaching experiences in public and private school contexts with marginalized communities.

Justin Garrick is head of school at the Canberra Grammar School in Australia. He completed his PhD at the University of Cambridge and holds an MBA from the University of London. Justin is a board member of the Association of Independent Schools in both the Australian Capital Territory and New South Wales.

Rafał Piwowarski is professor of educational policy at the Maria Grzegorzewska University, Warsaw, Poland. His scholarly interests include educational research referring to school locations, access to education, student achievements, and teacher prestige. He is the author of several books and numerous scholarly articles. Between 2007 and 2015, Dr. Piwowarski was the national project manager of the international project TALIS, devoted to teachers and school principals.

Jack Rice is the director of the Center for Montessori Education and a Lecturer in Educational Leadership at Loyola University Maryland. Jack has been named to the 2019–2020 cohort of the Academy of Innovative Higher Education Leadership, hosted by Georgetown and Arizona State Universities.

Abebayehu Tekleselassie is associate professor of educational administration at the George Washington University. His work has appeared in many peer-reviewed journals including *Leadership and Policy in Schools*, *International Journal of Educational Development*, and *International Studies in Educational Administration*. Dr. Tekleselassie was a U.S. Fulbright Scholar to Ethiopia in the 2014–2015 Academic Year.

About the Editor

Peter R. Litchka is professor of educational leadership at Loyola University Maryland, where he has been since 2006. Prior to coming to Loyola, Peter was in public education for thirty-three years, including being a classroom teacher, a school and district administrator, and twice a superintendent of schools in New York state. He is author/coauthor of three books in educational leadership, numerous scholarly articles, and has presented in the United States as well as in Canada, Cyprus, Israel, Poland, and Turkey. Peter received his bachelor's degree from the State University of New York at Geneseo, his master's degree from Johns Hopkins University, and his doctorate from Seton Hall University. He is currently president of the International Society for Educational Planning.

Other books by Peter Litchka:

The Dark Side of Educational Leadership: Superintendents and the Professional Victim Syndrome (with Walter Polka, 2008)
Living on the Horns of Dilemmas: Superintendents, Politics and Decision-Making (with Walter Polka and Frank Calzi, 2014)
Exemplary Leadership Practices: Learning from the Past to Enhance Future School Leadership (2016)
School Leadership That Works: Ideas from Around the World (2019, editor)
Serving Unique Populations: An International Perspective on School Leadership (2019, editor).

www.ingramcontent.com/pod-product-compliance
Lightning Source LLC
Chambersburg PA
CBHW051815230426
43672CB00012B/2749